THE MEDICINE BOWS
Wyoming's Mountain Country

THE MEDICINE BOWS

Wyoming's Mountain Country

By

SCOTT THYBONY
ROBERT G. ROSENBERG
ELIZABETH MULLETT ROSENBERG

The CAXTON PRINTERS, Ltd.
Caldwell, Idaho
1985

Library of Congress Cataloging in Publication Data

Thybony, Scott.
  The Medicine Bows.

  Bibliograpy: p.
  1. Medicine Bow National Forest (Wyo.) — History.
I. Rosenberg, Robert G. II. Rosenberg, Elizabeth
Mullett. III. Title.
F767.M43T49   1985   978.7'86   85-4152
ISBN 0-87004-308-0

Printed and bound in the United States of America by
The Caxton Printers, Ltd.
Caldwell, Idaho 83605
142223

DEDICATION

For Erik and Andrew, whose lives
will make the next chapter.

CONTENTS

		Page
PREFACE	. . . .	xv
INTRODUCTION	. . . .	xvii
	The Place	xviii
	Time Depth	xix
	Medicine and Bows: Notes on the Name .	xix
I.	EARLY MAN IN THE MOUNTAINS	1
	Mountain Refuge	3
	A High Country Way of Life	5
II.	THE MOUNTED HUNTERS	6
	Warfare	6
	Hunting	10
	Vision Quest	13
III.	THE TRIBES	17
	The Shoshone	20
	Arapaho	25
	The Cherokee Trail	30
IV.	THE MEDICINE BOW FRONTIER	32
	Early Exploration and the Fur Trade . . .	32
	Explorers from Washington	35
	Overland Trail	40
	The Union Pacific	43
V.	THE NATIONAL FOREST	46
	Creation and Consolidation	46
	Early Rangers	49

Page

VI. BROADAX AND PICKAROON:
THE LOGGING INDUSTRY 55
Before the Rangers: Pre-1902 55
Union Pacific Railroad 59
Coe and Carter 61
The Carbon Timber Company 63
The End of an Era: Logging, 1915 to Present 68

VII. THE LIFE OF THE TIE HACK 77

VIII. FIRE PREVENTION 87

IX. PICK AND SHOVEL:
THE MINING INDUSTRY 93
Gold on Douglas Creek 94
The Gold Hill Boom 97
Cooper Hill Prospects 101
Centennial Ridge Mines 101
Copper in the Sierra Madres 104
The Rudefeha or Ferris-Haggarty Mine . 105
Mining Camps in the Encampment District 106
Waning Days of the Ferris-Haggarty Mine . 109
Mining Around Laramie Peak 111

X. THE SHEPHERD AND THE COWBOY . . 113
Grazing on the Forest 114

XI. GETTING FROM HERE TO THERE 122
Trail 122
Road 124
Rail 136

XII. FIGHTING THE DEPRESSION:
CIVILIAN CONSERVATION CORPS 139

XIII. TAKING TO THE HILLS 146
Resorts and Lodges 146
Environment as Education 152
Winter Sports 153

Page

XIV. WATER 156
      The Forest as Watershed 156
      Water for Cheyenne 159
      Conclusion 161

BIBLIOGRAPHY 163
APPENDIX 171
INDEX 173

ILLUSTRATIONS

Page

A possible timber lodge on Elkhorn Creek. 9

Sioux woman. 19

Shoshone Sun Dancers, Western Wyoming, 1895. 21

Shoshone mother and child, Reservation Period. 23

Medicine man blessing sun dancer about 1904. 27

Painted buffalo skull near Sun Dance grounds. 29

"Laramie Peak from LaBonte" from the diary of Robert Clarke (1868). . 34

Army covered wagons at work on Pole Mountain. 48

Early forest rangers like young Ranger Henry
had to be skillful with horses 51

A young George Hilton is pictured in a field of pasque flowers. . . 54

The tie hack hews his tie with a broad ax. 56

Government sawmill near Laramie Peak, 1863–1865. 57

Devils Gate Camp and Landing of the Carbon Timber Company. . 65

Timber flume of the Carbon Timber Company on Devils Gate. . . . 65

Skidding logs to a portable sawmill. 69

Headquarters of the Carbon Timber Company at Keystone. 71

A portable sawmill operation. 73

Employees of the Wyoming Timber Company break up a landing. . 73

Pike poles are used to dismantle the landing for a tie drive. 74

Breaking out a landing on Douglas Creek for the 1928 drive. . . . 75

A typical tie hack's cabin. 77

Tie hack "tools of the trade." 78

A suitable lodgepole pine is being sawed by a tie hack. 79

After felling the tree, the tie hack clears it of limbs. 80

With an 8 foot pole, the tie hack measures off the length of a tie. . 81

The tie hack scores two surfaces with a double-bladed ax. 81

A tie hack hewing a tie with his broad ax. 82

Tie hack peeling the bark from the tie with a "spud peeler." 82

The bark is peeled off the underside with a spud peeler. 83

By using a pickaroon, the tie hack is able to skid the tie
     along the ground to the skid road. 83

A drive of ties and saw logs jammed on Douglas Creek. 85

Bull chain and boom at Ft. Steele. 85

Ranger E. J. Williams and helpers haul map board, linoleum
     and supplies up Medicine Bow Peak to the fire lookout. 87

Lookout's cabin at Lookout Lake. 88

Medicine Bow Peak Lookout. 89

Rangers toil up Medicine Bow Peak under the weight of
     telephone poles. 90

Lorraine Lindaley (1921) was the first female fire lookout. 91

Firefighters battle Turpin Creek blaze in 1915. 92

Holmes mining camp. 93

Keystone mining community in 1906. 96

A twenty-stamp mill was constructed in 1890 at Keystone. 96

The Little Florence Claim near the Keystone mining district, 1925. . 97

Many Scandinavians came to the Medicine Bows as tie hacks. 98

The mill at Gold Hill in 1900. 99

The mining town of Battle in the Sierra Madres. 108

A Basin Land and Livestock Company outfit. 115

The Ralston cabin. 115

Sheep operator E. Stratton and family, 1926. 116

Day-old lambs and their mothers enjoy the summer range. 117

Ranger Defler counts in a flock of sheep. 118

Branding calves on the Medicine Bow National Forest, spring, 1922. . 119

Sheepherders in Wyoming were often French or Basque immigrants. . 120

Snowy Range Road. 125

Snowy Range Road. 127

Page

Early campers enjoy the Forest with an elaborate camp. 128

This eight-pound trout was caught in Lake Marie in July, 1920. . . 129

An early version of the four-wheel drive. 131

Ranger Williams clears felled timber. 132

A telephone construction crew takes a break. 141

Medicine Bow National Forest hosted several CCC camps. 142

Early road work in the forest. 143

Libby Lodge (Snowy Range Lodge), 1927. 147

Medicine Bow Lodge, built in 1917, featured a main lodge
and numerous small cabins. 149

Ranger Williams plants trout in a high mountain stream. 157

PREFACE

WRITING A HISTORY of the Medicine Bow National Forest creates its own history. In the summer of 1981, the U.S. Forest Service contracted with Archeological Services to prepare an overview of the cultural resources of the Medicine Bow National Forest and the Thunder Basin National Grassland. The overview was to be used in the preparation of a comprehensive management plan for the forest. The cultural resource contract was eventually completed by High Plains Consultants, Inc.

The authors worked on the initial overview for High Plains during the fall and winter of 1981–1982. It became apparent during this study that a convenient history of the Medicine Bow region was not available to the general public. With the encouragement and support of High Plains Consultants and the Forest Service, the authors undertook to write a nontechnical history of the forest from prehistoric times to the present, based on the original overview.

A project of this sort must make demands on the knowledge, resources, and patience of a great many people. We were continually shown consideration by busy individuals in a manner that exceeded our expectations and their job descriptions. In particular we would like to acknowledge the help of Art Leys and the Medicine Bow National Forest staff, and Emmett Chisum and Paula McDougal of the American Heritage Center, University of Wyoming.

— Scott Thybony, Robert G. Rosenberg,
and Elizabeth Mullett Rosenberg

INTRODUCTION

THE HORIZONTAL FORCE of the Great Plains begins to weaken when the Wyoming border is reached, and the vertical starts to take hold — slowly at first and then more abruptly. Three long fingers of mountain reach north from Colorado into the southeastern corner of Wyoming: the Laramie Range on the east, then the Medicine Bow Range, and finally the Sierra Madre Range on the west. Largely forested, major portions of these ranges are now part of the Medicine Bow National Forest. Between these, the land is open and still plains-like.

For plains-living Indians, this high, wooded country was a place of mystery. Their geography of the supernatural peopled the mountains with spirits and powerful mythological events, creating an environment well suited for their vision quests. It was also dangerous country. Forest and broken country provided good cover for an enemy, increasing the chances of a surprise attack. In the mountains the horse was also less effective, reducing speed and mobility which hampered their fighting and hunting abilities.

The early pioneers were more at home in the mountainous country and soon began to translate the natural forces of the uplands into an economic reality. The mountain men trapped out the beaver, miners discovered good prospects, railroad men found their first source of ties since leaving Missouri, and the sheep and cattle men were able to develop good summer ranges.

Mountain and plains. Coming to terms with the mix of these forces has shaped the character of the people living in the Medicine Bow region. It is this character and the evolving resourcefulness of the people who have chosen to live in this unique environment that forms the history of the Medicine Bow National Forest.

The Place

Early descriptions of the Medicine Bow region vary as widely as the moods of the travelers who first saw it. After exploring the Great Basin country in 1850, Captain Howard Stansbury headed east and was inspired by the abundance of water and trees he found between the Sierra Madres and the Medicine Bows.

> Day after day, week after week, had we journeyed over that desolate basin, without a tree to be seen in the whole horizon. But now the rustling sound of embowering leaves assured us that we had once more reached a spot fitted by nature for the habitation of man (Stansbury 1852:240).

A few years before, Francis Parkman formed a different impression after reaching the eastern foothills of the Laramine Range.

> If a curse had been pronounced upon the land, it could not have worn an aspect more forlorn (Parkman 1849:172).

Being a region of extremes in topography and extremes in climate, the landscape brought out extremes in the way people felt about it.

The Medicine Bow National Forest is a vertical world. Only a short horizontal distance separates grassland from tundra. The highest peaks, up to 12,013 feet in elevation, can generate sudden snow storms at all times of the year. Over two hundred inches of snowfall is recorded annually for certain areas of the mountains, while the lower basins average only forty to sixty inches. Winters in the high country tend to be long and often severe.

There have been dramatic changes in the environment of the Medicine Bow National Forest over the past ten thousand years which are likely to have affected people living in the region. The climate has cycled between colder/wetter periods and warmer/drier ones. These fluctuations have resulted in glacial formation and disappearance in the high country and changes in the lower and upper treeline elevations. These shifting ecozones produced changes in mammal grazing patterns and the strategies of the prehistoric peoples hunting them (Grasso 1982:22).

Time Depth

People have lived in the region for over eleven thousand years and there is evidence they have been in the national forest for over eight thousand years. But how continuously man has occupied the mountainous areas of the Medicine Bow National Forest is unknown. There are no excavated sites within the forest and no clear sequence of occupation. From surface finds alone it is evident that people were using the forest by late Paleo-Indian times, about eight thousand five hundred years ago, and into historic times.

By the early 1800s when the first American explorers were pushing into the region, the Plains Indians had acquired both horse and gun, and had developed the classic culture of the mounted buffalo hunter. In historic times the region was never controlled by a single tribe. Between the Laramie Range on the east and the Sierra Madres to the west, the area was well known as dangerous and disputed country, where hunting and raiding parties entered at their own risk.

Medicine and Bows: Notes on a Name

The origin of the name Medicine Bow is still a mystery. It was first applied to the mountains, then the river, then the town made famous in Owen Wister's *The Virginian,* and eventually was given to the national forest. One of the earliest explanations of the name was recorded in 1899 by the historian, C. G. Coutant, who credited traditional sources. He said that northern tribes were known to come each year to the base of the Medicine Bow Mountains to gather a variety of ash for making bows. "Medicine" was interpreted as meaning excellent, so the name was thought to refer to the place where excellent bows could be procured. Lewis Hickman, an early settler who had been in the region since the 1850s, told a similar story. He said the name was given to the stream where big powwows were held, and where wood was gathered for bows. Other writers have presented the same idea, although the actual bow wood has varied in different accounts. Mountain mahagony and mountain birch are two favorites.

The word "medicine" was more commonly used by the plains tribes in reference to something powerful in a sacred way. An early ethnographer, Captain W. P. Clark (1885:428), said medicine could denote "holiness, mystery, spirits, luck, visions, dreams, prophecies," or "the concealed and obscure forces of nature, which work for good or evil." So, a medicine bow would have qualities beyond those normally associated with an excellent bow.

Ash and mountain mahagony were both used by Indians to make bows, but there are now no good sources of these woods in the Medicine Bow Mountains. Another possibility is cedar. An early rancher reported that a straight-grained, "white mountain cedar," which grew in only one location in the mountains, was used by the Indians to make bows. He mentioned he had once seen a bow made from it (Burns et al. 1955). Cedar is known to have been used for bows by the Plains Indians and the Shoshone, and has the advantage of not requiring seasoning before use. It was also used ceremonially by many tribes of the area for various purposes.

The Arapaho Indians called the Medicine Bows "the Hammer Mountains," referring to the stone hammers used in driving tent pins. The name may refer to the quartzite found in the mountains, and which may have been a source of hammerstone material.

THE MEDICINE BOWS
Wyoming's Mountain Country

I.

EARLY MAN IN THE MOUNTAINS

WHILE BELIEF among many archeologists is growing that man was present in the New World over 25,000 years ago, some of the oldest, undisputed evidence of Paleo-Indians in the Northwestern Plains comes from the Colby site near Worland, Wyoming. This is a mammoth kill site dating 11,200 years old, where fluted Clovis points were found. The Union Pacific Mammoth site close to Rawlins is another Clovis period site located near the Medicine Bow region.

It is not known to what extent these mammoth hunters used the higher country, but occasional surface finds of Clovis points are reported from a number of areas. They have been found in the Big Horn Mountains near timberline and one is reported from above timberline in the Colorado Front Range. The presence of a possible grinding stone at the Colby site and Clovis points in higher elevations and various ecological niches may point to a broad-spectrum hunting/gathering strategy for the early Paleo-Indian period. There are also numerous surface finds of a style of fluted point found at an elevation of eight thousand five hundred feet in a small area of the Big Horn Mountains. This point type may represent a transitional period between Clovis and Folsom.

With the extinction of the mammoth, a species of buffalo larger than the modern bison became the focus of the hunt. This change can be seen in the development of the fluted Folsom point, appearing about 10,700 years ago. While surface finds of Folsom points are common in the Northwestern Plains, occurrences in the high country are rare. At the Turk site on top of the Big Horn Mountains, there is evidence of Folsom point manufacturing, and two Folsom points have been reported above timberline in the Front Range. Folsom points are also reported to have been unearthed on the Wagoner Ranch just north of the Sierra Madre Mountains. During the remainder of the Paleo–Indian Period, evidence increases for the utilization and seasonal occupation of the mountain region. Indications of this new adaptation have come primarily from the mountain areas of northern Wyoming. This early use of the high country began a pattern of living which has lasted until historic times.

The presence of man in the Medicine Bow National Forest stretches back eight thousand five hundred years. Yet, the entire prehistoric record for this length of time is contained in a few small sites scattered across a wide area of forest and mountains. The first people known to have entered the forest had a unique style of making stone knives and lanceolate points known as the Cody Complex. Similar tools have been found at mass kill sites on the plains mixed with thick layers of buffalo bone. These people were herd hunters who required close cooperation, at least during the buffalo hunting season. In order to control the direction of a buffalo herd's flight, it was necessary to orchestrate effectively the level of fear in the herd. This involved a large number of people working closely together. A herd might be driven up an arroyo without an exit or into the loose sand of a steep dune where the buffalo could be more easily killed.

The plains and intermountain basins may not have supplied the needs of these hunters consistently. They may have been such successful hunters, that the herds were thinned to the point they could not be driven, or a drier cycle of weather may have had the same effect. From the evidence recovered in the high country, these hunters must have occasionally left the plains and basins, but for what reasons and for how long are not fully understood. Eden projectile points, two styles of Scottsbluff points, and the Cody knife are usually diagnostic artifacts for this period.

The best documented of the Paleo-Indian sites in the forest

is a Cody Complex site from the late Paleo-Indian Period. It is an interesting site since it is located above eight thousand feet, rare for such an old site when conditions in the high country were much colder, and it is over a half mile from permanent water. Since these sites are usually found close to permanent water, it may be that in a well-watered mountain environment, permanent water was not as important a factor in camp selection.

Mountain Refuge

For most of the mountainous areas of the region, the evidence of human occupation begins to increase as a major climatic shift known as the Altithermal made itself felt about seven thousand five hundred years ago. During this warmer, drier cycle, evidence of people in the short-grass plains at a distance from the mountains is almost non-existent. At the same time, human activity in the mountainous areas was increasing. A style of living began to develop which was less focused on a single animal like the buffalo. The tool styles from this period are distributed across a smaller geographic area than earlier forms and are often made from local, poorer quality material. People were settling into a smaller range of country and were learning to use it more intensively. Since most evidence for human occupation of the Northwestern Plains during this time comes from the higher elevations, it is suspected that the mountains provided refuge for groups from the plains.

During an exceptionally dry peak of the Altithermal, a group of people migrated into the Colorado Front Range. They constructed a series of drivelines across the high tundra ridges and began trapping mountain sheep during the summer. In winter they moved down to the foothills. The mountain foothills of northern Wyoming were also the winter base for other mountain sheep hunters during this period, but there is no evidence of their using drivelines or traps.

In the mountains of southern Wyoming, the archeological record for the Altithermal is, so far, missing. It was not until the seasons began to turn cooler and wetter around five thousand years ago that remains of people in the higher elevations of the forest are again found. The plains and intermountain basins also began to be reoccupied at this time, which may have coincided with renewed productivity of the shortgrass plains and an upswing in the numbers of buffalo.

It is not known if these shifts in climate, together with the population fluctuations throughout North America, were gradual or quick. When a way of living is fine-tuned to the seasons, even a gradual shift of a few degrees in temperature or an inch or two of rain will make itself felt, and major changes in human cultures can occur. Some researchers believe these changes were quicker, harder, and shorter than previously suspected. This would have caused a greater disruption among the groups of people living in the region. The higher elevations continued to be occupied throughout the Archaic and Late Prehistoric periods, and even into historic times. Small sites from the Middle Plains Archaic (5000 before present) through the Late Prehistoric (1500–500 BP) have been found in the Medicine Bow National Forest.

While other mountainous areas have produced evidence that people developed a specialized way of living tailored to the wide variety of plants and animals found there, the recorded sites in the forest are too few to give a clear indication of the subsistence patterns. The forest may have been used only as an occasional refuge during periodic fluctuations in the buffalo herds, or there may have been a few, scattered bands of people maintaining a high country way of life that left little in the way of archeological remains.

In the past, archeologists have considered the mountainous areas of the Northwestern Plains to be marginal to the main cultural patterns unfolding on the plains. Beginning in the late 1960s, though, well stratified sites were found and excavated at higher elevations that exhibited long occupation and cultural adaptation independent of the plains. During this same period, the belief that the Paleo-Indian cultures were completely dependent on big game was questioned, raising the possibility of early use of higher ecological zones. Studies by Frison (1978) in the Big Horn Basin and surrounding mountains, Benedict and Olsen (1978) in the Colorado Front Range, and Wright, Bender, and Reeve (1980) in the Teton Mountains have demonstrated the existence of mountain and foothill oriented cultures since late Paleo-Indian times.

A High Country Way of Life

The movement into the higher elevations during the late Paleo-Indian Period required more than a shift in location. It also required a shift in subsistence strategies to match the greater variety of available resources. A group would winter in the lower foothills and hunt to supplement their stored food until edible plants were again available in the spring. The group would then move slowly up in elevation through spring and summer, keeping contact with whatever plant community was at its peak of productivity. Based on analogy from known hunter/gatherer societies, the men continued to hunt throughout the year, while the women would do the bulk of the plant gathering.

While large game animals roughly followed a similar schedule, they were not the prime reason for a group to be at a certain elevation at a particular time of year. Since the location of game animals was not as predictable as the location of edible plants, base camps would be located near one or more useable plant communities.

II.

THE MOUNTED HUNTERS

THE NORTHERN ARAPAHO, Northern Cheyenne, and Oglala Sioux were often found in the Medicine Bow region during historic times. They were mounted hunters, highly dependent on the buffalo. The Eastern Shoshone and the White River Ute, also frequently reported in the area, were mounted hunters, but with less dependence on buffalo. There were striking differences among the historic tribes in the region, but there were also great similarities in methods of warfare, hunting, and religion.

Warfare

In September 1850, an exploring party commanded by Captain Howard Stansbury and guided by Jim Bridger crossed the Laramie Plains from the west. As they neared the Laramie River, a herd of buffalo scattered through the low hills in front of them, and soon mounted Indians were seen in the distance. Stansbury ordered his men into a grove of cottonwoods where rough breastworks were quickly constructed. Since approaching the Sierra Madre Mountains a week before, the party had been on constant alert for war parties, and had been under orders to sleep with their weapons at night.

The Indians were seen approaching in considerable numbers, but they did not launch an immediate attack. As both sides waited, Bridger shouldered his rifle and walked forward while making signs to the Indians. He was quickly recognized, and the Indians began racing up to the cottonwood grove with outstretched hands trying to shake with everyone they could find.

These Indians turned out to be a village of several hundred Oglala Sioux and some Cheyenne that had left Fort Laramie to escape an outbreak of smallpox. While hunting buffalo in the rich Laramie Plains, they had mistaken Stansbury's group for their enemies, the Crow Indians.

Food was soon served to the unexpected guests, as was customary, and a pipe of friendship was passed. Although Bridger did not speak either Sioux or Cheyenne, he began telling a story in sign language.

> He held the whole circle, for more than an hour, perfectly enchained and evidently most deeply interested in a conversation and narrative, the whole of which was carried on without the utterance of a single word. The simultaneous exclamations of surprise or interest, and the occasional bursts of hearty laughter, showed that the whole party perfectly understood not only the theme, but the minutiae of the pantomine exhibited before them (Stansbury 1852:254).

Although fighting was averted in this case due to Bridger's diplomacy and the fact that the Oglala had recently signed the Treaty of Fort Laramie, warfare was a common occurrence in the region.

The eighteenth and nineteenth centuries produced widespread tribal migrations and almost constant warfare. Access to hunting territories was often dependent on military force, while male prestige and wealth in horses was usually linked to success in war. With the acquisition of the horse and gun, new military patterns emerged which caused the old, settled ways of living and growing crops to become a liability. Many of the plains tribes had previously been occasional farmers, but became nomadic hunters within several generations. A nomadic village was more difficult to raid and less rewarding. To increase protection against raids, large nomadic villages became more common. This further increased dependence on the buffalo, a resource rich enough to support large populations. The overwhelming dependence on the buffalo was well recognized by some American military officers who advocated extermination of the buffalo as a means of defeating the tribes.

This new pattern of mounted, nomadic buffalo hunting required a good supply of horses. While raiding was common, trading seems to have been a more dependable method of acquiring horses in the early horse days. During the 1700s, the Shoshone, one of the first Northwestern Plains tribes to possess the horse, were constantly raiding other tribes for slaves to be traded to the Spanish for horses.

Whenever one group possessed military superiority, pitched battles were rare. The well-armed Blackfeet eventually forced their Shoshone enemies into adopting guerilla warfare tactics. The Shoshone waged a defensive war while looking for an opportunity to attack smaller, isolated groups of the Blackfeet. Essentially, this same pattern of hit-and-run raiding was continued by the Plains Indians when confronted by the overwhelming firepower of the Americans. The Indians rarely entered into a large-scale engagement without possessing a superior force.

Confronted by what appeared to be a hostile party of Indians, Stansbury "forted up." His men quickly built a rough breastwork of available material which was a standard technique used by Indians and whites when confronted by a numerically superior enemy. Early accounts from the region show its widespread use. The party of Arapaho that met Robert Stuart at the north end of the Laramie Range in 1812 built two "breastworks of logs" to stay in for the night. Rufus Sage, an early trapper, reported three "Indian forts" on the head of Rock Creek in 1842, and John C. Fremont a year later saw three "strong Indian forts," recently occupied, on the upper west fork of Laramie River. Forts were also reported in the Laramie Range and on the Medicine Bow River. When Stansbury crossed the North Platte above Saratoga, he found twenty conical timber lodges, which he called "Indian forts or lodges." These timber lodges were commonly used by the Plains Indian war parties, while similar structures were used by the Utes on hunting trips and by the Sheepeater Shoshone as summer lodges. A timber lodge has also been found in the Medicine Bow National Forest along the North Platte River.

The largest recorded battle in the region was at Fraeb's

Fort, reported to have taken place at the junction of Battle Creek and the Little Snake River (Hafen 1929). Fraeb and several trappers were killed there along with a number of Sioux, Cheyenne, and Arapaho.

Another fight was described by Clarence Tupper, a tie hack who had worked on the construction of the Snowy Range Lodge. He stated that an Indian raid was directed against an early mining camp called Silver City, situated where the lodge now stands, and at least one person was killed.

In 1869 Indians attacked a wagon train escort near Laramie Peak, killing one soldier and wounding another, and in 1874 two soldiers were killed guarding the lumber train from the government sawmill near Laramie Peak. A trapper by the name of John Pullum, a member of the Bean-Sinclair party from Arkansas, was also reported killed by the Gros Ventre on what is probably Jack Creek in the Sierra Madres sometime before 1844 (Fremont 1845:281).

Paul J. McKillip

A possible timber lodge on Elkhorn Creek, Medicine Bow National Forest. A number of timber lodges are also reported in North Park.

There were, no doubt, numerous battles between hostile groups of Indians in the area which were never recorded. There is one report, though, of a battle between the Sioux and Ute in 1856 on Pass Creek (Medicine Bow Forest Collection), and mention of a fight between the Sioux and Shoshone (possibly Ute) in the Medicine Bow Mountains.

Hunting

The link between man and buffalo on the Northwestern Plains has been strong since Paleo-Indian times. Cooperative hunting of buffalo by large groups of people occurred in the area for over eleven thousand years. Styles of hunting changed and the range of the buffalo fluctuated, but the basic communal hunting pattern persisted through historic times.

With the increase in buffalo herds during a neo-glaciation called the Little Ice Age, roughly A.D. 1400 to A.D. 1800, and the acquisition of the horse during the latter half of that period, the rewards of the mounted buffalo hunter increased tremendously. Greater mobility enabled fewer men to range farther, take greater numbers of buffalo, and transport them home more easily. This increased efficiency provided the Plains Indians with a degree of affluence unknown among many hunter/gatherers.

By the early 1800s, the basic technique for hunting buffalo on horseback was the surround. This technique was witnessed by Francis Parkman in 1846 when he accompanied a band of Oglala Sioux on a hunt near the base of the Medicine Bow Range. They were probably camped somewhere on Rock Creek when scouts reported buffalo to the west. The men in the camp quickly grabbed their weapons and rode out of the village, with Parkman joining them. "All was haste and eagerness," he reported. "Each hunter whipped on his horse, as if anxious to be the first to reach the game."

After riding steadily for an hour and a half, they saw scouts in the distance signaling that buffalo had been discovered.

They soon reached the ridge where the scouts were stationed and readied their equipment.

> . . . some thirty of the hunters galloped away towards the left, in order to make a circuit under cover of the hills, that the buffalo might be assailed on both sides at once. The rest impatiently waited until time enough had elapsed for their companions to reach the required position. Then, riding upward in a body, we gained the ridge of the hill, and for the first time came in sight of the buffalo on the plain beyond.
>
> . . . each hunter, as if by a common impulse, violently struck his horse, each horse sprang forward, and, scattering in the charge in order to assail the entire herd at once, we all rushed headlong upon the buffalo. We were among them in an instant. Amid the trampling and the yells I could see their dark figures running hither and thither through clouds of dust, and the horsemen darting in pursuit.
>
> While we were charging on one side, our companions attacked the bewildered and panic-stricken herd on the other. The uproar and confusion lasted but a moment. The dust cleared away, and the buffalo could be seen scattering as from a common centre, flying over the plain singly, or in long files and small compact bodies, while behind them followed the Indians, riding at furious speed, and yelling as they launched arrow after arrow into their sides. The carcasses were strewn thickly over the ground (Parkman 1849:216-222).

Even though the gun was widespread among the Plains Indians at this time and was used extensively in war, the bow and arrow was preferred for hunting buffalo. On horseback at close range, it proved the most efficient hunting weapon until the introduction of the repeating rifle.

Hunting in the mountains followed a different pattern, usually involving only individuals or small groups. Toward the end of winter when dried buffalo meat ran low, the Eastern Shoshone would hunt elk, deer, mountain sheep, and occasionally mountain bison by driving them into deep snow with dogs. They would also use dogs to corner mountain sheep in areas where they could subsequently be shot. While traveling through the Laramie Range, sixty to seventy Sioux once spotted a herd of mountain sheep and went after them on foot. But only a half-dozen sheep were killed during the afternoon's hunt, which may be one reason why the Sioux concentrated their attentions on buffalo. Elk was the most important meat source after buffalo for many of the Plains tribes. They would be hunted year around as the opportunity afforded. There is also some evidence for cooperative hunting in the mountains. Three game traps were found in northwestern Wyoming that may have been used by the Shoshone.

Sharing of the kill is widespread among hunting/gathering people. There are times when even good hunters are unsuccessful, so a tradition of sharing, with implied reciprocity, is important to the survival of the group. Often the hunter was entitled only to the hide and other choice parts with the remainder going to those in need. When Stansbury ascended the west flank of the Laramie Range, he found his own hunters butchering a buffalo which they had recently killed. A half-dozen Sioux who had claimed a share were also helping with the butchering.

The sharing of food with guests is also an established custom among hunter/gatherers, and the guest is usually obliged to eat what is served. The Shoshone, like many Americans, could not stomach boiled puppy — a delicacy among many plains tribes. Although every part of the buffalo was used at one time or another by the Plains Indians, waste seems to have been common in times of plenty. Stansbury was shocked to see the dried carcasses of buffalo stewn about the Laramie Plains, with only the choice parts butchered and the rest left to the scavengers.

The Medicine Bow region was well known for its herds of buffalo and other game. The plains and parks were rich in buffalo, while large herds were reported in the Laramie Range. Buffalo bones have also been found high in the Medicine Bows. Many travelers before 1850 commented on the quantity of game in the region throughout the year, but later ranchers thought the buffalo must have gone lower to avoid the harsh winters. William H. Ashley, though, in 1825 reported "innumerable herds of buffalo, antelope and mountain sheep" while traversing along the base of the Medicine Bow Range in mid-winter (Dale 1941:129). In 1831–1832 Zenas Leonard and other trappers of Captain Stephens' party wintered on the Laramie Plains and were able to live off the buffalo and other game in the vicinity. The buffalo were gone from the region by at least 1868, having already disappeared west of the Divide by 1840. A small number of mountain bison lingered in the high country a few more years; one was spotted in North Park in 1895, another was killed on Big Bull Mountain in 1900.

While the Plains Indians hunted a wide variety of animals and had an extensive knowledge of wild plants, they were still dependent on one primary food source. Dependence on one animal is risky for a hunting/gathering society. The threat of starvation for buffalo hunters was especially great since the number of buffalo was dependent on the cyclic nature of the short-grass plains, and their migration routes were unpredictable. Throughout the 1800s there were numerous reports of near starvation among the plains tribes. When the Oglalas told Stansbury they had left Fort Laramie to avoid smallpox, it may have been as much a fear of starvation as a fear of the disease itself. If enough of the hunters were incapacitated by sickness, starvation would occur.

Most observers realized that the fate of the Plains Indian was interwoven with the buffalo and many predicted that with the end of the buffalo, the Plains Indian would also disappear. Although the Plains Indians have survived, the near extinction of the buffalo combined with military defeat and relocation in the 1880s effectively destroyed the integrity of the Plains Indian culture.

Vision Quest

After hunting buffalo near the Medicine Bow Mountains, Francis Parkman traveled with the Sioux back across the Laramie Plains. After a day spent resting, Parkman decided to wander into the Laramie Mountains to escape the monotony of camp.

Walking for some time, he spotted an Indian in the distance who turned out to be his friend, Mene-Seela.

> As I had approached noiselessly with my moccasoned (*sic*) feet, the old man was quite unconscious of my presence; and turning to a point where I could gain an unobstructed view of him, I saw him seated alone, immovable as a statue, among the rocks and trees. His face was turned upward, and his eyes seemed riveted on a pine-tree springing from a cleft in the precipice above. The crest of the pine was swaying to and fro in the wind, and its long limbs waved slowly up and down, as if the tree had life. Looking for a while at the old man, I was satisfied that he was engaged in an act of worship, or prayer, or communion of some kind with a supernatural being (Parkman 1849:269).

There was a general belief among the Indians that the sacred was not abstract and distant, but alive in every facet of nature. The sacred could manifest itself through natural forces like the thunder, wind, sun, and moon, and through natural beings like the bear, antelope, and eagle. They also believed that an individual could make direct contact with the supernatural and so acquire the personal power necessary for success in life.

The acquisition of power took various forms, the most important being the vision quest. Around puberty a boy was instructed in proper conduct and the necessary approach to the sacred by either a shaman or, among the Shoshone, a relative. He would then undertake a vision quest, usually choosing a high, isolated place where the sacred was thought to be near at hand. Preparation for a vision quest might involve fasting, sweat baths, cold water immersions, or self-inflicted wounds. The Sioux would sometimes construct an enclosed pit to heighten sensory deprivation and increase the chance of a vision. The individual undertaking a vision quest would remain alone for several days until he had a dream or vision where a certain animal would appear and give advice, a song, or a certain ritual to follow. The vision experience would become his power, or medicine, for the rest of his life, and the animal would become a guardian spirit. Among females the acquisition of supernatural power was usually not as formalized and often occurred through dreams.

Parkman (1849) recounts a story told by an old Indian of a vision quest which was undertaken somewhere in the Laramie Mountains. As a young man, the Indian had gone into the mountains and found a cave. With his face painted black, he lay fasting and praying for several days until an antelope appeared. This was considered by the Oglala to be a peace spirit, and it returned a number of times. Finally the antelope spoke, telling the young man he was not to go to war, that his power would instead come from giving counsel to his people. This was considered an unusual vision among the Sioux, since a vision quest often provided the power necessary for success in war.

The vision quest played a more limited role among the Arapaho than most Plains tribes. The few that sought visions did so well past puberty and would keep their experience secret. Around the age of forty-five, they would formally present their vision to the religious leaders to be sanctioned.

While the probability is high that many areas of the forest were used for vision quests, no evidence has been uncovered that a specific area or terrain feature was considered more sacred than others.

There is a local belief that the Vedauwoo rocks were considered a sacred area by the Indians. The name is an Arapaho word which was translated as "earth born" by the Rev. John Roberts, an early missionary at Fort Washakie. The name was borrowed from Robert's word list by Mabelle Land Dekay as the title for a play she wrote. The play, *Vedauwoo, A Pageant-Drama Based on Fact and Fancy,* was performed in 1924 by the University of Wyoming Theater Department in a natural amphitheater of the Vedauwoo rocks. That area became associated with the play and subsequently was referred to by the play's name, Vedauwoo.

One area that was held sacred by various tribes in the region is the springs at Saratoga. John H. Mullison, one of the early Medicine Bow rangers, said the springs were considered "big medicine," and the mountain man, Jim Baker, said they were used for curing. The Indians would enter the hot springs and then jump in the cold river. When this treatment was used for smallpox, though, many of the Indians died and the springs then acquired a reputation as "bad medicine." Both Baker and Mullison stated that the area around the spring was considered neutral ground by the Indian tribes.

III.

THE TRIBES

AS EARLY AS 1876, the commanding officer at Fort Sanders near the present day city of Laramie, believed the Indian troubles had ended. He credited General George Crook's offensive in the Big Horn country for drawing the Indians away from the Medicine Bow region. But patrols were still being sent out through 1878, and in 1880 soldiers were ordered to intercept three hundred Indians reported by settlers in North Park to be in the area. The scare was short-lived as the Indians were only on a hunting trip.

Even after the Indians had been removed to reservations, they were still encountered in the area. As late as 1890, a small group of Indians, using a travois, were traveling along a branch of the Cherokee Trail at the north end of the Medicine Bow Mountains. When three deer ran across the trail and into a small grove of aspen, the men grabbed their rifles and sat down on the leeward side of the grove. The women circled the trees, lighting fires on three sides. The deer were soon flushed out, but the grove and surrounding rangeland were badly burned (Burns et al. 1955).

The major tribes using the region during historic times were the loosely allied Northern Arapaho, Northern Cheyenne, and Oglala Sioux, and also the Eastern Shoshone, and the White River Utes. Territorial claims by the various tribes were often exaggerated, overlapping, and never secured by sustained use or military superiority.

What constituted the actual territory of mounted nomadic hunters dependent on migrating herds, constantly displaced by warfare, and subjected to intense cultural pressures from an expanding American frontier is difficult to say. Early mapmakers usually settled for printing a tribe's name in boldface letters across a huge geographic area. But even when the information they obtained from traders and explorers was accurate, it was quickly dated.

A tribe consisted of several autonomous bands often operating under their own leaders. The exploitive net of a band would be spread as wide as security and resources allowed. This range was extended even farther by individual parties traveling great distances for war, trade, and small-scale hunting and gathering. During historic times, a small party from any of the major tribes in the region might be encountered from Mexico to Canada.

After 1800 the Medicine Bow region fell outside what would be considered the home territories of the tribes that used it. The core area for the northern bands of Arapaho and Cheyenne from the early 1800s to the early 1860s was generally east of the Laramie Range between the North and South Platte Rivers, although a number of winter camps were made outside this area. The eastern bands of the Shoshone were generally centered in the Green River and Wind River region, while the core area of the Oglala Sioux was north of the North Platte. The White River Ute were generally found southwest of the Sierra Madre Mountains.

The region was well known for hunting, raiding, and trading. The Sioux and Cheyenne hunted extensively in the Laramie Plains and the Laramie Range, while the Arapaho pushed even farther into the mountain parks. Although generally oriented to the plains, the Arapaho were called "mountain Indians" by their close allies, the Cheyenne, since certain bands spent a good deal of the year in the higher elevations. The Shoshone hunted buffalo on the western Laramie Plains and one band wintered along the upper North Platte Valley, possibly as far up as North Park. The Utes pushed up from the south into the Little Snake River country and into the upper North Platte region, where they frequented the Encampment River area and lower French Creek. The Crow occasionally dropped down from

Courtesy American Heritage Center, University of Wyoming *Charles F. Guild*

Sioux woman. Between 1830 and 1870 the Sioux were frequently reported in the Medicine Bow region.

the north to hunt and raid in the Laramie Plains, and there were even isolated reports of Gros Ventre and Pawnees in the region. Sometime before 1841, the Arikara, a Missouri River tribe, raided horses from a party of trappers near the base of the Medicine Bow Mountains. The Arikara were known to have spent the years 1832–1837 hunting from the forks of the Platte River to the mountains (Denig 1950). This disperal from their river villages was caused by crop failure, Sioux raids, and the scarcity of buffalo. The Arikara also attacked a party of trappers in the Laramie Range in 1833. Combined with the pre-1800 accounts of Comanche, Kiowa, Kiowa-Apache, and Plains Apache, the region presents an intricate cultural mosaic.

As representative of the major tribes of the Medicine Bow, the way of life of the Shoshone and the Arapaho, as seen through early accounts from the region, will be presented in greater detail.

The Shoshone

The Shoshone, commonly referred to as the Snakes in historical accounts, seem to have entered the Northwestern Plains from the Great Basin. Both linguistic and archeological evidence suggests an arrival in southwestern Wyoming by the 15th century. The Comanche split off from the Shoshone and moved eastward during this period, while the Shoshone pushed to the northeast. The Shoshone may have been in the Laramie Range area during the 16th to 17th centuries, but the main thrust of their expansion was further north.

The Shoshone and Comanche were among the first groups on the Northwestern Plains to possess horses, probably acquiring them between 1690 and 1700. At least one band of Comanche, the Yamparika, were in the mountains and plains of southern Wyoming from the mid-1700s to as late as 1790. This band was eventually forced south by armed enemies, possibly the Kiowa who had a tradition of driving the Comanche south from the Black Hills country prior to 1790. By 1800, within a single generation, the Shoshone were pushed back from the plains to an area west of the Continental Divide by a combination of better armed enemies and smallpox.

The Shoshone maintained contact with the Spanish settlements to the south and made periodic trading trips by way of the upper North Platte and the mountain parks in Colorado. Lewis and Clark were told of a trade route used by the Shoshone which may have been this same one, and the Shoshone are believed to have traveled south along this mountain trade route in 1811 and 1826 (Hyde 1959). The best archeological evidence for the Shoshonean presence in the Medicine Bow region is a ceramic style known as Intermountain Ware. This style of pottery has been found at sites in the Laramie Plains, northern Colorado, and frequently in the Red Desert. Diagnostic Shoshone artifacts have not yet been reported for the Medicine Bow National Forest.

One of the first forest rangers in the Medicine Bow region was John H. Mullison who arrived in the area in 1868. At one

Courtesy American Heritage Center
Shoshone Sun Dancers, Western Wyoming, 1895.

time he worked as a post trader among the Utes who told him that during the winter of 1840-1841 an allied band of two thousand five hundred "Snakes, Shoshoni, and Bannock" wintered along the North Platte from the crossing of the Union Pacific Railroad south to the Colorado border. This group claimed as its territory the surrounding forest and the country from the source of the North Platte north to the Seminoe Mountains. That winter was said to have been exceptionally hard, with the snow four to five feet deep and crusted by early in the new year. Most of the buffalo and other game in the area died, while starvation combined with smallpox were reported to have killed one thousand eight hundred of the Indians. Due to this disaster, the area was considered bad medicine by the Shoshone, and abandoned. For the next ten years, the Utes and Arapaho fought over this region (Mullison and Lovejoy 1909). A similar killing winter was reported to have occurred on the Laramie Plains in 1844–1845 (Dodge 1877). Since these accounts are both second-hand, they may refer to the same winter.

Around 1843 a war party of Oglala Sioux caught two Indians (accounts vary as to whether they were Shoshone or Ute) in the Medicine Bow Mountains, killing one outright and capturing the other. The prisoner was scalped alive and then burned to death. Two years later the Shoshone destroyed a war party of ten Oglalas on the Laramie Plains. This almost precipitated an all-out war with the Sioux. To avoid it, the Shoshone returned the scalp of the chief's son with a parcel of tobacco tied to it. If the Sioux had been appeased, the custom was for the tribes involved to exchange gifts and adopt children from each other's tribe. The Shoshone gesture was not accepted, but the war did not materialize due to feuding among the Sioux and the skillful diplomacy of the traders whose profit would have been hurt by a general war.

The Shoshone were still claiming the territory around the Medicine Bow Mountains in 1850. By 1863, though, this claim extended only as far as the North Platte River and included the Sierra Madre Mountains. After this period, the

Courtesy American Heritage Center
Shoshone mother and child, Reservation Period.

major focus of the Eastern Shoshone shifted progressively north to the Wind River Basin.

The Eastern Shoshone annual subsistence cycle revolved around the fall buffalo hunt. The four dispersed bands would gather together in the Wyoming Basin and then travel east of the Divide to hunt. They would then pack the dried buffalo meat back to winter camps, usually in the Bridger Basin or Wind River Valley, and would remain there until late February or early March. Winter camps would break up and rendezvous for the shorter spring buffalo hunt, after which they would scatter into the higher country to hunt and fish in small groups. The summer and early fall were an important time for gathering roots and berries.

The White River Utes were also dispersed during the summer. Both the Utes and the Shoshone may have adopted this pattern since their enemies, the Plains Indians, were strongest during the summer when they gathered in large numbers for their tribal hunt and ceremonies.

With the Shoshone pulling back and the Arapaho generally east of the Divide, the Utes began pushing further north into the Medicine Bow region. From the 1850s to 1880 they frequented the North Platte and Little Snake drainages. In 1868 a Ute war party killed three tie hacks near Indian Creek in the Saratoga Valley. A year later, a party of Utes visited North Park and then spent a couple of months in the Denver area on their way to hunt buffalo.

In 1879 Major Thomas T. Thornburgh, who was killed in battle with the Utes a few months later, investigated a complaint from Agent Nathan Meeker that a party of Utes had deliberately set fire to the forest in the Sierra Madre Mountains and North Park area. He found that a party of one hundred Utes had appeared at a mining camp on the divide between Jack and Savery Creeks to trade, but they were peaceful, had set no fires, and had then headed south into North Park.

Arapaho

The Arapaho began their westward migration from central Minnesota and by A.D. 1700 had reached the mouth of the Little Missouri River. They were in the Black Hills country by 1730 and encountered the Cheyenne there around 1800. The Sioux were the last of the Plains tribes to cross the Missouri River and were exerting considerable pressure on the tribes farther west. This pressure forced the Arapaho to move south from the Black Hills, followed by the Cheyenne. Bands of both the Arapaho and Cheyenne eventually reached the Arkansas River country, while other bands remained in the north between the South and North Platte Rivers.

Robert Stuart and six Astorians intended to winter-over in 1812 at the north end of the Laramie Range on the North Platte, where they were discovered by a war party of twenty-three Arapaho. The war party was on its way north to raid the Crow Indians and, being on foot, intended to ride captured horses back. They told Stuart their village was on the South Platte. During this same period, Ezekial Williams and a party of trappers traveled south from the Big Horn country. Their exact route is unknown, but it is possible they crossed the Medicine Bows at one point. Part of the group eventually reached the South Park area where several trappers were killed by Arapaho.

The Arapaho were also reported responsible for the death of a trapper around 1821. Jacque La Ramie, a French-Canadian, wintered alone on the Laramie River and was killed, either at the mouth of Sybille Creek or farther upstream on the Laramie River.

These occasional reports of war parties are the only information available on the winter use of the region by the Arapaho. Rufus Sage, who trapped the area, considered the region dangerous only between May and November, while William H. Ashley and a company of his trappers passed through the area in the winter of 1825 without encountering any Indians. In addition,

Captain Stephens and his party of trappers wintered on the Laramie Plains in 1831–1832 without reporting any Indians. A possible explanation for the lack of winter use of the region, at least during post-horse times, is that the wrong variety of cottonwood grew in the area. The inner bark of cottonwood was often fed to horses during the winter when the grass was poor. Horses, though, would only eat what was known as sweet cottonwood, not the bitter type. Ashley found only the bitter variety when crossing the Laramie Plains. The Stephens party discovered this fact too late and lost all their horses which forced them to make two unsuccessful attempts to walk to Santa Fe from their winter camp on the Laramie River.

The Arapaho had the capability to winter in the higher elevations, having wintered in several of the mountain parks in Colorado and using snowshoes for hunting buffalo. The lack of winter use of the Medicine Bow region by the Arapaho may have been due to an inability to sustain large horse herds in the area.

The Arapaho are reported to have driven game through a gap known as "the door" where hunters were stationed to kill the animals as they ran through (Toll 1962). This was where the North Platte "crosses the Medicine Bow Range," and is probably located somewhere in North Gate Canyon. John C. Fremont came across a recently abandoned Arapaho village in this area in 1844. A clay used for blue paint by the Arapaho was also obtained in the vicinity.

The normal seasonal pattern of the Northern Arapaho was for the four bands to separate after the summer hunt and sun dance, and then move into their winter camp. This was usually within five to thirty miles of each other. Their winter camp was chosen at a wooded place in the foothills with good grass and plenty of water and game. The area between the bands was considered a game preserve where no individual hunters were allowed to hunt. The soldier societies would police the area, occasionally herding a small group of buffalo so they could be taken without scaring off the rest. In spring the bands

V. C. Trenholm Collection, American Heritage Center, University of Wyoming

Medicine man blessing sun dancer about 1904. The Sun Dance and tribal buffalo hunt were the focus of many Plains tribes.

moved as separate units down onto the plains to hunt antelope, eventually regrouping for the tribal buffalo hunt.

The Arapaho were still frequenting the source of the Platte River in 1830. The Sioux, though, generally stayed above the North Platte until the establishment of Fort William (later Fort Laramie) at the mouth of the Laramie River in 1834. This post was built to attract the trade of the Sioux, Cheyenne, and Arapaho. It was successful, and by 1840 the Sioux were hunting west of the Laramie Range. During this period, the Sioux formed an alliance with the Cheyenne which often involved the Arapaho, since they were allies of the Cheyenne. A Sioux war party attacked a small group of trappers near the headwaters of the Medicine Bow River in 1841, and later in the year attacked a party of Henry Fraeb's trappers at Five Buttes, west of the Sierra Madres. Jim Baker and several others trailed the Sioux eastward until the Indians reached their "stronghold" on the Laramie Plains. A few days later a combined force of Sioux, Cheyenne, and Arapaho attacked Fraeb's party and their Shoshone allies.

Raiding parties of Sioux, Cheyenne, and Arapaho were reported throughout the region for the next thirty-five years. In 1862 the Overland Stage route was relocated through Arapaho country in order to avoid Sioux raids to the north. Following the massacre at Sand Creek, Colorado, the Arapaho joined the Sioux and Cheyenne in reprisals throughout the region. After attacking the town of Julesburg on the Platte in 1865, the Arapaho were forced by intense military pressure to seek refuge in the Powder River country. This began a pattern of wintering in the north and summering in the Medicine Bow region. Throughout 1865 and again in 1867, there were numerous raids along the Overland Trail.

In 1867, the Pawnee battalion of the U.S. Army patrolled across the Laramie Range as far as the Laramie Plains to protect survey parties of the Union Pacific Railroad.

There were probably many Arapaho trails that crossed the Laramie Range. Of those that are still known, one followed up the ridge between the north and south forks of Lodgepole

Courtesy American Heritage Center, University of Wyoming
Painted buffalo skull near Sun Dance grounds.

Creek near Pole Mountain. Another generally followed Arapaho Creek in the Laramie Peak area.

Hostilities by the Arapaho and their allies continued in the region until the mid-1870s when military operations forced a permanent shift to the north. After 1877 the Arapaho frequently served as scouts and in the 1880s were organized into a formal U.S. Army unit with flag, uniforms, and white officers.

The Cherokee Trail

Travel over the mountains of the region has always been limited, but the adjacent basins and plains have provided several important routes. Skirting north of the Medicine Bow and Sierra Madre mountains was a section of a major trail system connecting the plains to the east with the Great Basin to the west. Parts of this eventually became known as the Cherokee Trail and then later, the Overland Trail. To the south, the Little Snake River served as an important route into the Green River, Great Basin, and Ute country in northwestern Colorado, while trails crossed the Laramie Plains leading southeast to the base of the Colorado Front Range and major north–south routes. The North Platte River provided access to North Park where trails led farther south into Middle and South Parks, and eventually to the Arkansas and Rio Grande Rivers.

When reports of the 1849 gold discoveries in California reached the Cherokee settlements in the Oklahoma/Arkansas border area, an expedition was organized under Captain Lewis Evans. This group of highly acculturated Cherokees traveled west in wagons and maintained a steady correspondence with their homes and the local Cherokee newspaper. When they reached Greenhorn, Colorado, near Pueblo, the party split up. Most sold their wagons and bought pack horses; others kept their wagons and went north to intersect the Mormon route on the North Platte. The pack horse party hired a guide named Owens who had been a member of Fremont's exploring party. Their route closely paralleled Fremont's 1843 route as far as the North Platte, and eventually became known as the Cherokee Trail. Cherokees were still using this route as late as 1852.

The Fremont route the Cherokees followed was, at least in part, already an Indian trail. Fremont followed a large Indian trail between the Cache la Poudre and Laramie Rivers, and when he crossed the Medicine Bow Range south of Elk Mountain, he found a broad trail, recently traveled, leading through the pass. Rufus Sage in 1841 called this the "pass-trail." When Lt. Francis T. Bryan traveled through in 1856, he located an Indian trail along the right (north) bank of Pass Creek, a very rough wagon road above Pass Creek on the north, and a pack trail that avoided Pass Creek Canyon. This pack trail was what was known to local residents as the "Cherokee Pack Trail" which crossed Oberg Pass.

IV.

THE MEDICINE BOW FRONTIER

THE MEDICINE BOW region was first exploited by Euro–Americans for its natural resources: the pelt of the beaver which inhabited its waterways, mineral wealth in the form of gold and silver wrested from the heart of its mountain chains, and the green carpeting of timber which covered those ranges on the edge of the plains.

Starting in the 1840s, the explorations of the Corps of Topographical Engineers sought to reconnoitre the vast western expanses, known only to the Indians and the mountain men, in order to create a system of forts, roads, and telegraph lines to bind the nation together from ocean to ocean. What was to become Wyoming Territory lay directly in the path chosen for the great westward migration and the first transcontinental railroad. The following chapters will discuss the important role of the Medicine Bow region in the unfolding national pageant of "manifest destiny" — the exploration, exploitation, and settlement of the western frontier.

Early Explorations and the Fur Trade

Although no actual evidence exists of direct Spanish contact within present day Wyoming, historians have continued to speculate on this possibility due to the proximity of documented expeditions in Colorado, Nebraska, and Utah. C. G. Coutant discussed the possibility of Spanish exploration in his *History of Wyoming* (1899:23–32). He admitted that the evidence was inconclusive, and urged other historians to pursue the subject further. Coutant mentioned ruins of stone dwellings near Lake DeSmet (north of present day Buffalo), found by the Connor expedition in 1865 and judged to be over one hundred years old at the time of their discovery. A stone arrastre (for crushing ore) was found in 1866 about fifty miles southwest of Fort Phil Kearney. John H. Mullison, a ranger on the early Medicine Bow National Forest, left an account of early mining evidence in what is now Mullison Park. Mullison noted the remains in 1870 and judged one to be at least one hundred seventy-five years old at that time.

The French trappers penetrated into what is now Wyoming, although much controversy surrounds names and dates. Francis Beard shows a French map made in 1720, which is supposed to depict the Laramie and Medicine Bow Mountains and the Laramie Plains (Beard 1933:2; Homsher 1949:1).

The first Euro-Americans in the region may have been a small trapping party led by Ezekiel Williams in 1807 or 1808. Working for Manuel Lisa near the headwaters of the Yellowstone, the party was driven south by the Blackfeet. A few survivors came into the Medicine Bow region, crossed the Snowy Range, and continued into Colorado (Coutant 1899:70–73). Another version states that Williams followed the North Platte to its source in North Park in 1810 or 1811 (Homsher 1949:3–4).

Jacque La Ramie (La Rameé, Laramie) whose name has been liberally used throughout the region, is reported to have trapped in the area in 1817. He was killed in 1820 or 1821 after setting out by himself to trap along the Laramie River (Homsher 1949:4). Exact movements of various trapping parties are difficult to chronicle as the evidence is scant and often unreliable. Few mountain men were literate or predisposed to write accounts of their adventures. Stories passed by word of mouth and were often greatly enhanced to highlight the exploits of the particular storyteller.

In the summer of 1834, Kit Carson and a small party trapped the headwaters of the Laramie River and its tributaries. While hunting elk for camp meat, Carson was attacked by two grizzlies and forced to leave his weapon behind in a footrace to the nearest tree. Unsuccessful at dislodging Carson from his perch, one bear left, but the second proceeded to tear up aspen trees in wrath and frustration. After the second bear finally left, Carson hastened back to camp ". . . never having been so scared in my life" (Carter 1968:60–61).

In 1824 and 1825, General William Ashley led an expedition of trappers up the South Platte River to the vicinity of present day Fort Collins, Colorado. He traveled northward across the Laramie Range onto the Laramie Plains and proceeded along the east base of the Medicine Bow Range, attempting to find a westward crossing. The month of March was not advantageous to a successful crossing and

> . . . after an unremitting and severe labour of two days, we returned to our old encampment with the loss of some of my horses, and my men excessively fatigued. We found the snow to be from three to five feet in depth and so firmly settled as to render our passage through it wholly impracticable (Dale 1918:129).

This unsuccessful crossing may have been attempted by way of the Little Laramie River. Ashley then proceeded around

"Laramie Peak from LaBonte" from the diary of Robert Clarke (1868) owned by Mrs. H. A. Furlong.

the north end of the Medicine Bow Mountains and Elk Mountain, then northwest out of the region. Controversy surrounds a trapper named La Bonte who gained fame from George Frederick Ruxton's *Life in the Far West* (1847). He was one of the principal characters in this historical fictional account of trapping in the early west. Historians Leroy Hafen and Bernard DeVoto, however, did not think La Bonte ever actually existed. La Bonte Creek and "La Bonte Camp" are mentioned in early accounts. The names La Bonte and David La Bonte also appear in traders' correspondence. It is fairly certain that there was a La Bonte Camp near the confluence of the North Platte River and La Bonte Creek, but there is not enough evidence to sketch in any details about the trapper La Bonte (Homsher 1949:5–6; Leonard 1972:1–26).

Explorers from Washington

Fremont: 1843

In 1843, the "Pathfinder," John C. Fremont of the Corps of Topographical Engineers, followed Ashley's general route through the study area. Guided by Tom Fitzpatrick and later accompanied by Kit Carson, Fremont set out with thirty-nine seasoned "Creole and Canadian voyageurs," a train of twelve carts, one light wagon, and a twelve-pound howitzer. A year earlier, Fremont had proceeded up the South Platte River to Fort St. Vrain, then traveled north to Fort Laramie along the east base of the Front Range and the Laramie Mountains. In 1843, he attempted to penetrate the Front Range and find a suitable passage westward for emigrant travel. It is interesting to note how few men were familiar with this particular area at this relatively late date. Fremont explains:

> It is singular that, immediately at the foot of the mountains, I could find no one sufficiently acquainted with them to guide us to the plains at their western base; but the race of trappers, who formerly lived in their recesses, has almost entirely disappeared — dwindled to a few scattered individuals — some one or two

of whom are regularly killed in the course of each year by the Indians (Fremont 1845:120).

Fremont had to employ the service of Alexis Godoy as guide, even though he had two of the most famous mountain men (Carson and Fitzpatrick) already in his party. They attempted to follow the Cache La Poudre River upstream but eventually headed northward through mountains and foothills to enter the Laramie Plains from the west. They camped on the Laramie River on July 31, and traveled across the Laramie Plains along the east base of the Medicine Bow Mountains. They camped on the Medicine Bow River on August 2 near "Medicine Butte" (Elk Mountain), passed to the south of Elk Mountain, crossed the North Platte River and then proceeded in a northwesterly direction to the Sweetwater River and South Pass (Fremont 1845:125–127).

In 1844, Fremont once again entered the Medicine Bow region from the west on his return from California. He followed the Elkhead (Little Snake) River and St. Vrain's Fork (Savery Creek) into the southwest portion of the Sierra Madre Mountains. He came within a short distance of the site of the Fraeb battle of 1841 (discussed below). He may have ascended Battle Creek, but whatever route he used, he reached the divide and descended a stream he called "Pullam's Fork," named after a trapper killed there by Gros Ventre Indians. He reached the North Platte River and turned southward, traveling through the three mountain parks of Colorado (Fremont 1845:281).

Fremont's chief contribution was conscientiously to record and map his travels. This information was used for many years by those who followed. He also tapped the memories of the remaining fur trappers and recorded their information for posterity. As Goetzmann states, "This was one difficulty with the specialized geographical knowledge which the mountain man possessed: it could die with him" (Goetzmann 1966:89).

In 1837 or 1838, Henry Fraeb [Frapp or Frappe) and Jim Bridger built a trading post on St. Vrain's Fork (Savery Creek) in the foothills of the Sierra Madres. Apparently this general region was not often trapped by the mountain men until the late 1830s, because it was heavily used by the Indians. Fraeb was an experienced mountain man and had been a partner in the Rocky Mountain Fur Company. He then went into business with Peter Sarpy and built Fort Jackson on the South Platte River. In 1841 Bridger was building the fort that would bear his name on Black's Fork and became concerned about Fraeb. He dispatched a search party that included Jim Baker.

Fraeb, meanwhile, was on a buffalo hunt and received news of an attack on a party of trappers near Five Buttes, resulting in the deaths of two trappers and the loss of one hundred head of horses.

Two weeks after receiving news of the action at Five Buttes, and after Baker's arrival, Fraeb encountered a large group of Indians. He sought protection in the log fortifications he had built on the north bank of the Little Snake River near Battle Mountain (formerly known as Bastion Mountain). This locality was near Battle Creek and Squaw Mountain, all subsequently named for the fight which ensued. The battle lasted several hours and resulted in Fraeb's death and that of seven or eight trappers. An estimated forty Indians were killed or wounded (Barnhart 1969:36–37; Stansbury 1853:239–240).

Stansbury: 1850

Portions of what would become the Overland Trail had been traveled by Ashley in 1825, and Fremont in 1843. Additionally, at least two emigrant parties had crossed in 1849. The Evans party, led by Captain Lewis Evans of Arkansas, was composed of a group of Cherokees either heading for the California gold fields or attempting to find new lands on which to settle. That year the Jones party crossed in the same vicinity, but no details are available. However, the value of this route as a possible alternative to the more northerly Oregon Trail was first officially recognized in 1850 by Captain Howard Stansbury of the Corps of Topographical Engineers. Stansbury, upon completion of an exploration and survey of the Salt Lake Valley, stated:

> It has been determined not to return by the beaten track, but to endeavor to ascertain the practicability of some more direct route than now traveled to the waters of the Atlantic. If it should prove to be practicable to carry a road across the north fork of the Platte, near the Medicine Bow Butte [Elk Mountain], and, skirting the southern limit of the Laramie Plains, to cross the Black Hills [Laramie Range] in the vicinity of the heads of Lodge-pole Creek, and to descend that stream to its junction with the South Fork of the Platte, nearly a straight line would thus be accomplished from Fort Bridger (Stansbury 1853:229).

Guided by James Bridger, Stansbury cut almost directly east from Fort Bridger on September 10, ascended Bitter Creek, and crossed Haystack Flats and the southern Red Desert region. Stansbury continued over Bridger's Pass (just north of the forest boundary in the Sierra Madres), crossed the North Platte, and stayed north of Medicine Bow Butte (Elk Mountain); whereas Fremont had turned south. He entered and crossed the Laramie Plains where he encountered a camp of Sioux and Cheyenne consisting of nearly one hundred lodges (Stansbury 1853:252–255). Bridger was well known to the Indians, and they camped peacefully within two miles of the village.

Stansbury attempted to cross the Laramie Mountains, but when he reached the crest and surveyed the route down Lodgepole Creek, it appeared too steep and heavily forested to use. Stansbury thought the range was more gentle to the south and would provide a better crossing point. He proceeded south-southeast, slowly descending until he struck a branch of Crow Creek. Stansbury apparently wandered among the hills for the rest of his descent until he picked up another branch of Crow Creek and reached the plains. He then turned north to reach Lodgepole Creek, which he intended to follow east to the forks of the Platte. He passed through "Cheyenne Pass" which he described as a depression about four miles wide between the Laramie range on the west and a plateau on the east. He finally reached Lodgepole Creek, but an injury prevented him from exploring it, and he was forced to seek aid at Fort Laramie (Stansbury 1853:259–261).

Stansbury felt that this new route was feasible for wagon emigration and would save approximately sixty-one miles between Fort Laramie and Fort Bridger. Eventually it was heavily utilized by emigrants; Ben Holladay realized its merits, and in 1862, relocated the Overland Mail route on it.

Bryan: 1856

In 1856, Lt. F. T. Bryan was ordered to find a suitable wagon road from Fort Riley, Kansas, to the Salt Lake Valley, utilizing Bridger's Pass. At this time, the federal government was concerned with what it considered the growing Mormon problem and the possibility of open conflict. Bryan traveled west as far as Bridger's Pass to determine the feasibility of Stansbury's route for wagon travel. Bryan ascended Lodgepole Creek into the Laramie Range, staying on a ridge formed between the two branches of that creek. He described it as ". . . exceedingly smooth and of a very gradual ascent, giving an excellent road" (U.S., Congress, Senate 1857:459). Bryan stated that he was following an Indian trail at this time, and that they obtained fine, straight lodgepoles in this area. Bryan had some difficulty in the last mile and a half before reaching the summit but found the descent "easy and gradual." He improved the route by moving boulders and cutting some timber to allow wagon passage. Bryan should be given credit for establishing a suitable emigrant crossing of the Laramie Range along the Lodgepole Trail, even though Stansbury had been through the same general area and initiated the idea.

Bryan crossed the Laramie Plains and once again skirted the mountains to the north. He camped on what he called the west branch of the Medicine Bon (Bow) and commented that this stream was "famous as a trapping ground for beaver." Bryan followed Pass Creek through the gap between the main range and Elk Mountain. At this point, he indicated that he was following an existing road and an Indian trail. Bryan also passed "an emigrant's grave (Pickens') at a good camping place" (U.S., Congress, Senate 1857:461–462).

It can be derived from his description that some kind of a road already existed, no matter how rough, and the description of the "emigrant" grave suggests that the trail had received some use. This road was probably the route laid down by Cherokee emigrant parties starting in 1849.

Finally, John Bartleson traveled eastward on the route in December 1857, under orders from Col. Albert S. Johnston to determine the feasibility of moving troops from Fort Bridger to Fort Laramie (U.S. Congress, Senate 1859). Randolph B. Marcy, who later wrote an emigrant guide for the U.S. Government, also crossed the route in 1858.

Overland Trail

Ben Holladay was granted the federal mail contract in March 1862 and used the existing Oregon Trail as his route. However, Indian depredations led him to the decision that a move southward might alleviate the problem. He utilized the Stansbury route, constructed a string of stations, and began service on July 21, 1862. It was called the Overland Stage Line, and the route became known as the Overland Trail (Hafen 1926:232). The route left the Oregon Trail and followed the South Platte River past Julesburg. It then crossed the prairie of eastern Colorado to Latham (near Greeley), where it turned northwest and followed the Cache La Poudre River to Laporte (north of Fort Collins). From Laporte it followed modern U.S. Route 287, crossing the Laramie Range to the Laramie Plains where it picked up the general route of Stansbury. It proceeded around the north end of the Medicine Bows and skirted north of Elk Mountain, crossed the North Platte River and the northern extreme of the Sierra Madres via Bridger's Pass to points west.

In the Medicine Bow area, the following stage stations were established (from east to west): Big Laramie, Little Laramie, Cooper Creek, Rock Creek, Medicine Bow, Elk Mountain, Pass Creek, North Platte, Sage Creek, Pine Grove, Bridger's Pass, and Sulphur Springs.

Stage stations were located at ten to fifteen mile intervals. Teams were changed at the "swing" stations, but no services were provided for passengers. The swing stations consisted simply of a stable and granary, with small adjoining living quarters for the stock tenders. Two men generally manned each of these stations. A fresh team in harness was ready for the arrival of the stage, and could be changed in about fifteen minutes while passengers stretched their legs. The "home" stations, at fifty-mile intervals were more elaborate. Meals were provided for passengers and drivers were replaced. Telegraph communications were established between the stations. In periods of Indian peril, personnel with their stock from the intervening swing stations often sought protection at the home stations.

Stages were driven day and night, and two forty-minute stops were made for meals. The system of swing and home stations enabled a passenger to travel between one hundred and one hundred twenty-five miles in a twenty-four-hour period (under ideal conditions). Holladay charged passengers (as of 1866) $150 between Atchison and Denver, $300 to Salt Lake City, $450 to Nevada, and $500 to California (Rusling 1875:41–42).

In moving south, Holladay did avoid serious Indian troubles until 1865 (although the summer of 1863 brought several raids). In retaliation for the Chivington Massacre at Sand Creek, Colorado, Cheyenne allied with Sioux and Arapahoe raided Julesburg, Colorado, a major station and small settlement along the Overland Trail. Seventy-five miles of trail on either side were devastated. Several stage station operators, soldiers and emigrants were killed along the Overland Trail that summer, and several stations were burned. The portion of the route in the Medicine Bow region was considered the most dangerous. Robert Spotswood testified before the Senate in 1878: ". . . whenever a man left Virginia Dale and started on that break he was in danger of his life, for an Indian was likely to jump up from behind a bush at any point and shoot him down" (U.S. Congress, Senate 1880:47). Although hostilities slackened in 1866, the year 1867 witnessed more depredations along the Overland as a result of the Fetterman Massacre of December 21, 1866 and Red Cloud's war in the Powder River Basin.

The Peace Commission of 1867 met with the Indians for fifteen months and secured the relinquishment of the major Overland routes. More important, the Union Pacific Railroad had reached present-day Wyoming in 1867, and viewed as a larger threat, diverted the Indians' attention (Hafen 1926:322).

With the driving of the golden spike at Promontory Point on May 10, 1869, the Overland stage era was effectively ended, although emigrants continued to use the route for an undocumented period of time. This route has not received the fame of the Oregon Trail to the north, and its use as an emigrant trail has not been well recognized or recorded. However, Dr. J. H. Finfrock, post surgeon at Fort Halleck (near Elk Mountain on the Overland) recorded the passing of 17,584 emigrants and fifty thousand head of livestock in the year 1864 (Barnhart 1969:64), indicating that the Overland Trail was well used by emigrants. With Holladay's stage system in operation, the traveler was assured of at least limited military protection and regular water/aid stops at the stage stations.

Prior to the building of the first transcontinental railroad, the Overland Trail and its stage stations represented the main Euro-American presence in this region. However, this was a rather tenuous chain which was often broken by Indian attack. Protection was offered to travelers by the military presence at Fort Halleck and by roving detachments.

In 1866, Fort Sanders (originally called Fort John Buford) was constructed on the Laramie Plains, near present day Laramie, by Captain Henry R. Mizner. Built from the lumber of Fort Halleck which was abandoned at the same time, it was located on the Laramie River near the Overland Stage route and the Lodgepole Trail, and provided protection for both, being about six miles from the former and one mile from the latter. The soldiers stationed at Fort Sanders, the stage operators, and "a handful of people" were the only inhabitants in the region at this time (Homsher 1949: 13–14).

Politically, the region was still a part of the unorganized portion of the Louisana Purchase (1803). In 1834 it was officially labeled Indian Country, being outside any organized territory or state. It was administered by the Commissioner of Indian Affairs under the War Department. It retained this status until 1854 when it a became part of Nebraska Territory, thence Idaho Territory in 1863, and Dakota Territory in 1864. Finally, on July 25, 1868, it became the Territory of Wyoming (Barnhart 1969:5–6; Homsher 1949: 17–18).

The Union Pacific

The Union Pacific Railroad was the chief catalyst in opening the Medicine Bow region to settlement and exploration. It is interesting to speculate how the opening of this area may have been retarded if a different right-of-way had been chosen. As it was, early settlement patterns for the entire region were determined by one man, Grenville M. Dodge, the chief engineer for the Union Pacific Railroad Company. An interesting feature of the building of the Union Pacific was its construction through undeveloped country. Farther east, railroad systems developed between existing large population centers as the need arose. The result of the railroad construction in Wyoming was that early settlement, coal mining, commerce and ranching clustered along the right-of-way.

General Dodge had inspected the Laramie Mountains on his return from the Powder River expedition in 1865 to determine the feasibility of a railroad route through the area. Leaving his troops on the east side of the Laramie Range, he explored crossings which a railroad might negotiate. He followed Lodgepole Creek to the summit and turned south where he encountered a party of Indians. He was forced to stay on the crest until rescued by his troops. On his return to camp, he inadvertantly found the approach for which he had been searching (Dodge 1910:16–17; Homsher 1949:30–31).

When he became chief engineer in 1866, he rejected a southern route through Colorado as well as a more northerly route along the Oregon Trail. Although the northern route may have been gentler and better watered, it was more frequently subject to Indian attack, was somehat longer, and did not have coal reserves that were already known to exist along the central route. The central route was approved on November 23, 1866 (Homsher 1949:31).

Dodge was beset with engineering and logistical problems in addition to Indian attacks. There were power struggles with one of the directors of the company, Thomas Duran, who attempted to get Dodge replaced, as well as temporal pressures created by competition with the Central Pacific.

In the vicinity of what is now the Pole Mountain Division of the Medicine Bow National Forest, Dodge had to bridge the chasm over Dale Creek before descending to the Laramie Plains. This involved building a tremendous wooden trestle 126 feet high and about 720 feet in length, an engineering feat in 1867. The small community of Dale City grew up nearby to house the workers who constructed the bridge (Homsher 1949:34).

The following stations were established as the line advanced westward: Buford, Sherman (which acted as a repair shop and freight station), Dale City, Red Butte, Laramie City, Cooper Lake, Lookout, Miser, Rock Creek, and Como (Homsher 1949:34).

In 1867, Indian attacks and raids were common. Striking from Lodgepole Creek, the Indians harassed work crews by pulling up survey stakes and running off stock. In escalating violence, a railroad party was attacked and killed on the Laramie Plains. Another party lost a soldier and a tie hauler. In April 1868, a work party was audaciously attacked only four miles west of Fort Sanders; one man was killed and four were wounded (Homsher 1949:32–33).

Laramie City was established in May 1868 and Albany County was formed the following December. The permanence of Laramie was assured when it was chosen as the major railway division point and extensive machine and repair shops were built.

The impact of the Union Pacific on the settlement of the region was great. It provided the connections with markets to the east, vital for ranching development. It created the logging industry of the Medicine Bow National Forest by becoming the major market for railroad ties. The Union Pacific also bought and transported mine props for use in the coal mines managed by the Union Pacific Coal Company.

V.

THE NATIONAL FOREST

Creation and Consolidation

UNTIL THE FORMATION of the Medicine Bow National Forest in 1902, commercial use of the area was virtually unregulated. Logging, mining, and ranching interests exploited the natural resources of the region, unhampered by added cost or restrictions. Some timber and stock raising concerns felt threatened by the proposed administration of these lands by the United States Forest Service, and strongly protested its presence. Many area citizens, however, felt the need for the protection and preservation of resources that the government would provide, and petitioned President McKinley in 1899 to set aside the Medicine Bow area forests as a reserve, citing the ". . . wholesale stealing of timber by the companies." Powerful timber interests delayed the action until 1902 when the Medicine Bow Forest Reserve was established. The forest had far reaching and long range effects on all types of land use: logging, mining, grazing, irrigation, transportation, and recreation.

The original boundaries encompassed about two million acres of the Medicine Bow or Snowy Range. The east and west boundaries approximated those of the present Laramie and Brush Creek Districts; the northern boundary was south of the present one, and the southern boundary extended south into Colorado to the area around Estes Park (Bruce 1959:1).

In 1908, the forest was divided. The Colorado section was named the Medicine Bow Forest. The Wyoming section, including Crow Creek Forest Reserve (est. 1900) was named the Cheyenne National Forest. Two years later, the Colorado portion became known as the Colorado National Forest, and the Cheyenne National Forest became the Medicine Bow National

Forest (Medicine Bow Collection). This land represents about two-fifths of the Medicine Bow National Forest today.

In 1924, further boundary changes were made. Based on a survey conducted in 1909, some lands were eliminated, others added. An addition of 28,818 acres was made to the Medicine Bow Division, including Sheep Mountain, which was designated a National Game Refuge on October 8, 1924 (Medicine Bow Collection).

Until recently, the Medicine Bow Division consisted of four ranger districts: Centennial, Foxpark, Bow River, and Brush Creek. It is now administered through two ranger districts: the Laramie District, formed from the former Centennial, Foxpark and Pole Mountain districts, with its headquarters in Laramie; and the Brush Creek District, formed from the old Bow River and Brush Creek districts, with its headquarters in Saratoga.

The Hayden Division of the Medicine Bow National Forest was originally set aside as the Sierra Madre Forest Reserve on November 5, 1906. Two years later, the Sierra Madre Reserve and portions of the Park Range Forest Reserve (now part of the Routt National Forest in Colorado) were combined to form the Hayden National Forest. It was named for Dr. F. V. Hayden, the head of the U.S. Geological Survey in the Rocky Mountain area. On August 2, 1929, President Herbert Hoover dismantled the Hayden National Forest. The Colorado portion was added to Routt National Forest, while the Wyoming portion was added to the Medicine Bow National Forest as the Hayden Division (Medicine Bow Collection).

The Pole Mountain District was originally the Crow Creek Forest Reserve, established in 1900 by President William McKinley. Just three years later, an Executive Order designated that same land be used by the War Department, establishing the Fort D. A. Russell Target and Maneuver Reservation. Two years later, Cheyenne National Forest was created by combining Crow Creek National Forest and the Wyoming Division of Medicine Bow National Forest. On April 19, 1910, the Crow Creek Division of the Cheyenne National Forest was abolished, and the War Department took complete control. In 1925, the administration, protection, and resource development of the land was transferred back to the Forest Service, in cooperation with the War Department. With the exception of 3,317 central acres to be withheld as the Fort D. A. Russell Target and Maneuver Reservation, the Pole Mountain District of the Medicine Bow National Forest was established. On July 1, 1925, it was designated as a federal game refuge. In 1959, Fort Francis E. Warren (formerly Fort D. A. Russell) found the Pole Mountain Target and Maneuver Reservation in excess of its needs, and by 1961, all military interests on Pole Mountain were terminated. Boundaries have remained essentially the same, and encompass 55,908.99 acres. It is now administered as part of the Laramie District, with headquarters in Laramie.

The Laramie Peak Division was added to the Medicine Bow National Forest by an Act of Congress on August 20, 1935 with the assistance of Wyoming Senators Carey and O'Mahoney (Armstrong 1935:26). Intensive settlement of the Laramie Peak

Medicine Bow Collection — American Heritage Center
Army covered wagons at work on Pole Mountain, location of Fort D. A. Russell (now F. E. Warren) Target and Maneuver Reservation.

region began as a result of the 1916 Grazing Homestead Law which permitted the filing of 640-acre tracts. World War I veterans received residence credits based on military service, and rushed to claim vacant lands. Since the Laramie Peak area was a zone high in lightning-caused fires, the residents were anxious to receive aid from the Forest Service for fire fighting, especially since the area was an important watershed for the surrounding irrigated communities (Medicine Bow Collection).

Early Rangers

The Forest Service was transferred from the Department of the Interior to the Department of Agriculture on February 1, 1905, during the administration of Lewis G. Davis, the first supervisor of Medicine Bow National Forest. Forest policy was directed by Gifford Pinchot, the director of the U.S. Forest Service. The economic potential of the forests was recognized, and in the early years, grazing was regulated and fees charged. Also, trespass cases were filed against the many timber operations on forest property (Bruce 1959:8–10). Davis also authorized construction of a ranger station in Chimney Park and a small cabin on French Creek (Bruce 1959:16–17).

Two of the most colorful and influential early forest rangers were John H. Mullison and Louis E. Coughlin. Mullison was born in Pennsylvania in 1842. He was a veteran of the Civil War, having been captured by the rebels and imprisoned at Andersonville. He came west after the war and was the post trader at the White River Agency at Meeker, Colorado, in the late 1860s. He was reportedly well-liked by the Ute Indians at the agency and was warned by them to leave just before the Meeker Massacre. Unfortunately, the dates do not tally, as the famous massacre did not occur until September, 1879. He came to Wyoming in 1870, where he experienced life as a prospector, tie camp boss, and ranch hand (*Laramie Republican-Boomerang* 4/6/12).

Coughlin, known as the "dean of the forest rangers" in the Rocky Mountain region, worked for the Forest Service for over forty-five years. Coughlin was born on a cattle ranch in the Little Laramie Valley, and entered the Forest Service in 1908. Less than a year later he was assigned as district manager on the Battle Mountain District of what was then the Cheyenne National Forest, where he worked extensively with grazing. In the next few years he served on the Foxpark District and the Centennial District, where he was district ranger. In 1913, he was assigned to the Forest Supervisor's office in Laramie, where he served as office manager.

During his record breaking forty-five years of service, Coughlin was instrumental in establishing many improvements on the forest, including the establishment of the Somber Hill fire lookout in the Foxpark District and Medicine Bow Peak fire lookout, and construction of the Woods Creek Road and most of the trails in the Foxpark area. Coughlin's specialities were fire prevention and wildlife management. He strengthened game laws, established winter game surveys, and set up game check stations. He stepped up range management programs, reseeding, and research projects while in charge of Pole Mountain. He was also interested in beaver control and Christmas tree cultivation.

Coughlin was also the unofficial historian of the Medicine Bow National Forest. In the early 1950s, he compiled historical data from the beginning of the forest. He collected memos, letters, old reports, and corresponded with early personnel, asking them for their reminiscences. His letters indicate that he hoped to have a history of Medicine Bow completed in time for the fiftieth anniversary of the forest, which would have been in 1952. He did complete lengthy historical notes which are available in the Medicine Bow Collection, but never completed his comprehensive history. When he reached the age of 70, Coughlin was forced to retire from government service. He was never able to receive the financial or technical help needed for such a project, and it was therefore never completed. Coughlin died in 1962 in Laramie.

The second forest supervisor, succeeding Lewis Davis, was Jesse W. Nelson, who served from April 15, 1907 to June 30,

Early forest rangers like young Ranger Henry had to be skillful with horses; few had the luxury of motor vehicles.

1908. Nelson had been a ranger at Cody on the Shoshone National Forest and had proved himself a good grazing administrator. Grazing and timber were the two main concerns of his administration. He instigated stock counting, which was initially opposed by stockmen, and constructed wire corrals on each driveway at the forest boundaries. The first ranger stations on the Sierra Madre were constructed at Heather Creek and Big Creek, and a telephone line was built from Saratoga to Brush Creek and Keystone in 1908 (Medicine Bow Collection). Nelson's ability in range management was recognized, and he was promoted first to Washington, D.C., then to Denver as the Assistant District Forester in charge of grazing, leaving his post on the Medicine Bow on June 30, 1908 (Medicine Bow Collection).

Supervisor P. S. Lovejoy took office on July 1, 1908 and remained until June, 1911. Since the Sierra Madre Division had become the Hayden National Forest in 1908, Lovejoy was responsible only for the Medicine Bow and Pole Mountain divisions.

During his tenure, timber sales continued to the Carbon Timber Company. There was also a timber sale to the Laramie, Hahns Peak and Pacific Railroad along its right-of-way through the forest. Forest personnel continued their regulation of sheep and cattle grazing. Contruction was begun on the Snowy Range Road, a new station at Foxpark, cabins for the Bow District winter use, and various roads and trails. Lovejoy described the sheep industry as the leading economic factor in the forest, followed by hay, cattle, timber, and mining (Bruce 1959:29).

Christopher M. Granger was the fourth Medicine Bow supervisor, and served from June 1, 1911 to February 26, 1913. Timber and grazing continued to be the major concerns of the forest. The Carbon Timber Company was still operating and the forest was negotiating with it for settlement of a large timber trespass. As part of the settlement, the Carbon Timber Company built a fire line around the outer edges of the timber cut area, and much of the monetary settlement was used in the construction of telephone lines and a wagon road from Centennial via Sand Lake to the Medicine Bow Ranger Station. Most of the sheep grazing was supervised by the grazing ranger at Brooklyn Lake. Reductions were made in both sheep and cattle because of overgrazing. During his administration, ranger stations were constructed at Brush Creek and Bow River (Medicine Bow Collection).

The next forest supervisor was George A. Duthie, who served from March 1, 1913 to February 18, 1917. Those four years marked the transition from the era of the saddle horse and wagon to that of the automobile. By 1916 cars could be driven to Keystone, Foxpark, Brooklyn Lake, and Libby Flats. With the exception of Louis Coughlin, forest personnel neither owned nor could operate automobiles, and continued to use horses in their work. In 1913, the Medicine Bow National Forest (consisting at that time of just the main Medicine Bow Range) was divided into five ranger districts: Foxpark, Keystone, Brush Creek (Drinkhard), Bow Station and Seven-mile Station. In addition to the five rangers in charge of these districts, a sixth ranger was stationed at Brooklyn Lake to oversee sheep allotments, act as a general trouble shooter in the summers, and work in the Laramie office in the winters. This position had been filled by John H. Mullison, who died in 1913 and was succeeded by William F. Will (Duthie 1961:1–2).

At the beginning of Duthie's tenure, grazing was the chief business of the forest, and timber sales were at a low ebb. However, timbering picked up over the next few years because of available lumber from the Laramie, Hahns Peak and Pacific Railroad line and the formation of new timber companies and sawmills (Duthie 1916:3–4).

Forest communications depended mostly on the one hundred seventy-five miles of ground circuit telephone line. Roads and trails needed much improvement, and began to receive attention, both for better fire-fighting access and to encourage tourists. Recreational use of the forest was first developed around this time (Duthie 1916:8).

Huber C. Hilton served from 1921 to 1934 and had, with the exception of James Blackhall's twenty years as supervisor of the Hayden, the longest term in the Medicine Bow National Forest, remaining supervisor for over thirteen years. His lengthy

Medicine Bow Collection — American Heritage Center
A young George Hilton is photographed in a field of pasque flowers by his father,
Forest Supervisor H. C. Hilton, in 1925.

administration oversaw many changes and improvements. A great deal of road construction was completed, including the road across the Snowy Range (1925–1926). The CCC program was established in 1933, with seven camps of some five hundred men in or adjacent to Medicine Bow National Forest. Hayden National Forest became a division of the Medicine Bow (1929), and initial surveys and reports were completed on the Laramie Peak area, which became a division in 1935. Sheep Mountain and Pole Mountain were both added to the forest as federal game refuges. In 1934, Hilton was transferred to the regional office in Denver (Medicine Bow Collection).

See appendix for complete listing of Forest Supervisors.

VI.

BROADAX AND PICKAROON: THE LOGGING INDUSTRY

THE MEDICINE BOW region has been blessed with vast stands of lodgepole pine, a tree which grows straight and tall, tapers gradually and has a relatively clear bole. Even as the aboriginal populations took advantage of its attributes for their dwellings, the Euro-Americans utilized the lodgepole pine for the building of the first transcontinental telegraph and railroad. The Medicine Bow region provided the first important stands of timber needed for building material after the barren expanses of the prairie. Although the lodgepole pine furnished the basis for the railroad tie industry, it was also the source of material for building military installations, stage stations, towns and villages, bridges, ranches and fences, and cordwood to provide the most basic needs of heat for comfort and cooking.

Before the Ranger: Pre-1902

One of the earliest documented uses of what would become the Medicine Bow National Forest (Laramie Peak Division) was for the building of the transcontinental telegraph in 1861. The contract for the construction of the portion from Omaha to Salt Lake City was given to the Pacific Telegraph Company. Edward Creighton was the superintendent of construction. The route followed the Oregon Trail up the Platte and North Platte Rivers, passing through Fort Laramie and north of what would become the Laramie Peak Division of the forest along the Oregon Trail (Thompson 1947:361). This route was also used by Ben Holladay's Overland Mail service, as well as the Pony Express.

Medicine Bow Collection — American Heritage Center
The tie hack hews his tie with a broad ax, standing atop the tie.

Charles H. Brown was a member of the party that built the first transcontinental telegraph. In his diary, he described the constant search for poles while crossing the prairies to the east. About twenty to twenty-five poles were needed per mile. When advance parties reached the Laramie Peak region, abundant timber was found in the surrounding foothills. Camping near the Horseshoe Creek stage station (near present day Glendo), Brown and his party ". . . started early this morning with whole train for the foothills of Laramie Peak to cut telegraph poles. Our direction was a trifle west of south. The train wended its way up the creek, keeping in the valley thereof. . . . The train made only about eight miles before camping for dinner and cattle rest" (Brown 1861:60, 77). After dinner, Creighton and McCreary started on muleback to select a place to cut poles. They found poles in abundance and easily accessible at the base of Laramie Peak.

The train moved forward the following day and "in the afternoon all the men were busy cutting, peeling, and hauling out the poles for loading" (Brown 1861:79). By August 6, ". . . he (Jim Creighton, Edward's brother) had already cut

Drawn by Casper Collins
Government sawmill near Laramie Peak, 1863–1865.

and distributed from this point — the foothills of Laramie Peak — 1,075 number one poles and then cut and shaved, ready for hauling, about 450 more" (Brown 1881: 100–101). For Creighton's division four hundred men, three hundred head of oxen, mules, and one hundred wagons were used. Creighton and his men finished their section by October 19. The entire telegraph was finished five days later, slightly four months after the project had begun (Thompson 1947:66–67,363). It is likely that Creighton utilized other portions of the Laramie Peak District, but no other information has been uncovered.

Creighton and C. H. Hutton built a second telegraph line from Denver to Salt Lake City in 1865–1866 along the Overland Trail (Coutant, 1899:374). Ben Holladay had moved his Overland Mail route to this southern passage in 1862 in an attempt to lessen Indian depredations. It appears likely that poles for its construction were taken from the main Medicine Bow Division. It is documented that the system of swing and home stage stations along the Overland were built from locally-cut logs.

Fort Halleck was built near Elk Mountain in 1862 to house troops protecting the Overland route. T. B. Murdock, formerly a soldier at Fort Halleck, stated that he had helped construct the fort . . ." [we] built nearly all the quarters at Fort Halleck; chopped the logs, and hauled them down from the timber, and put them up; we hauled what timber there was in them from Laramie Peak" (U.S., Congress, Senate 1880:74). It would seem that Murdock was actually referring to Elk Mountain.

Fort Fred Steele was established in June 1868 along the North Platte River at the crossing of the Union Pacific Railroad. The surgeon's report for 1870 states:

> Stone was at first selected, but subsequent orders having been issued to use timber, parties were sent to Elk Mountain, before referred to, where large numbers of pine logs were cut, and drawn to the post. Two stream saw-mills were set up near the river, about half a mile from the post, and the logs prepared for buildings

(U.S. War Department, Surgeon General's Office Circular No. 4, Dec. 5, 1870:357–359).

Franklin Hess states that the sawmill was moved to Elk Mountain to facilitate work. Curious Indians were dispelled by blowing a steam whistle on the apparatus (*Laramie Daily Bulletin* 6/1/56).

The Laramie Peak District was used as a wood source by the Wyoming Central Railroad (part of the Chicago and Northwestern) when it was built from Nebraska through Lusk and Douglas (1886) and on to Casper to 1888. It is also possible that the Cheyenne and Northern Railroad tapped this area when it was constructed northward through Wheatland and on to Wendover in 1887. The Chicago, Burlington and Quincy Railroad was built from the Bighorn Basin through Wind River Canyon to Casper and reached Orin Junction in October 1914 (Larson 1965:159, 340). In a region generally surrounded by plains, the Laramie Peak District represented the only major wood supply for these railroads.

Union Pacific Railroad

The most extensive early lumbering operations within the present forest occurred during the construction of the transcontinental railroad across Wyoming. At least three companies contracted with the Union Pacific Railroad in 1867 to cut ties in the Laramie Mountains (first known as the Black Hills) prior to the actual construction the following spring. They were Gilman and Carter, Paxton and Turner, and Sprague, Davis and Company (Bratt 1921:162; Homsher 1949:57–58).

Gilman and Carter's main camp was moved west from Pine Bluffs to a point about one mile north of Fort Sanders in the fall of 1867. In June 1868, they established a camp two and one-half miles north of Sherman called Sherman Camp Station. Other tie camps were established south of Tie Siding, at Rock Creek, and at Medicine Bow along the Union Pacific right-of-way. An estimated several hundred thousand ties and one hundred thousand cords of firewood for steam engines were cut near Sherman Station and Tie Siding so that the tie contractors ". . . had stripped the hills and canyons for many miles north of Sherman and Tie Siding Stations . . ." (Bratt 1921:162).

Gilman and Carter was composed of two factions, the Gilman Brothers headed by John Gilman, and the Carter faction, composed of the partnership of Levi Carter and General Isaac Coe (Bratt 1921:136–137). In June 1868, Gilman and Carter took a contract to cut ties for the construction of the Denver Pacific Railway from Cheyenne to Denver. The ties were cut on the headwaters of the Cache La Poudre River in Colorado and driven downstream to the prairie. The Gilman faction did not believe the venture would prove profitable and attempted to withdraw from the agreement. Coe and Carter took over the entire contract which, in the end, netted $50,000 (Bratt 1921:153–154). As a result of the Denver Pacific episode, it was mutually agreed to dissolve the Gilman and Carter partnership; henceforth the two companies operated separately as the Gilman Brothers and Coe and Carter. The latter was to become the dominant force in the tie industry in Wyoming prior to the turn of the century.

Coe and Carter received handsome profits by paying 35 to 60 cents a tie and receiving $1.00 to $1.30 each from the Union Pacific (delivered) at Sherman Station, Fort Sanders, etc., along the right-of-way. For cordwood, they paid $6 to $8 per cord and received $12 to $16 per cord from the railroad (Bratt 1921:144).

Numerous local merchants in and around the new town of Laramie participated in the business of supplying the Union Pacific with ties. Prominent among them were Wilcox and Crout, Charley Bussard, J. S. McCool, Charley Hutton, the Dawson Brothers, Hance, and the Trabing Brothers. All of these interests participated in large "tie drives" down the Little and Big Laramie Rivers in the early 1870s, tapping the Snowy Range to the west.

These companies also cut lumber for the construction of the prairie railroad town (Homsher 1949:58–59).

Coe and Carter

According to Ranger John Mullison's history written for the *Forest Atlas* in 1909, Coe and Carter established tie camps along every drivable stream on the east side of the Snowy Range, and on Douglas and South French Creeks on the west side. Mullison estimated that three million ties were cut from the Medicine Bow from 1867–1870 for the Union Pacific. All ties were cut from lodgepole pine about 11–14 inches in diameter. About seventy-five thousand cords of wood were also cut. According to Mullison, the indiscriminate cutting and shoddy lumbering practices led to numerous forest fires. These fires were allowed to burn themselves out, which resulted in extensive erosion damage to the watershed (Mullison 1909:43–44).

Once the initial construction phase passed, prices for railroad ties dropped to about fifty cents for a first-class tie, and specifications increased from 6-x-6 inches to 7-x-7 inches. Cordwood fell to $6.50 per cord, delivered. Thus, when the tie industry stabilized and the day of quick and easy profits had passed, most small competitors were forced out of the business, and Coe and Carter prevailed. They soon provided nearly all the railroad ties for Wyoming, western Nebraska, and parts of Colorado (Mullison 1909:45–46).

At this time, the timber companies were under no government regulations and used the public domain and its resources free of charge. The commissioner of the General Land Office for the United States attempted to regulate the industry in the Wyoming Territory in October 1871, but it does not appear that these regulations were ever taken seriously by the large timber interests. In Albany County, a 16⅔ percent tax was levied on lumber. However, it was not popular with the general public and was dropped. Timber taxes remained an issue throughout the 1870s, but business appeared to continue as usual (Homsher 1949:61–62).

Coe and Carter continued operations on the Medicine Bow Range with camps on Rock Creek, Medicine Bow River, Brush Creek, and French Creek. Ties were floated down the North

Platte River to Fort Steele. A significant change in the lumber industry came in 1875 when the Rocky Mountain Coal Company was formed (essentially a subsidiary of the Union Pacific Railroad). Coal mines were located and exploited all along the right-of-way throughout Wyoming, and steam locomotives switched from wood to coal. The cord wood industry ended, but a new business in mine props began to take its place. From 1870 to 1880, Mullison estimates that 2.5 million ties and four hundred thousand mine props were cut, delivered, and sold, all from the Medicine Bow (Mullison 1909:46–47).

Louis Sederlin was an active logger on the north end of the Medicine Bow Mountains. In the summer of 1875, Sederlin and eight men bought four thousand ties from a chopper on Turpin Creek. They also cut ties during the winter of 1875–1876, and drove them that spring down Turpin Creek and the Medicine Bow River to Medicine Bow. Years later, Sederlin stated that he sold these ties to the Longmont Railroad (probably the Colorado Central) at forty-nine cents a tie. In 1881 or 1882, he built a sawmill near the John Anderson Ranch. He described it as a water powered gang sawmill. He charged twenty-five to twenty-seven cents per measured board foot (Medicine Bow Collection). Logs were hauled from the forest to a log chute built down a steep hillside and skidded down to the East Fork of the Medicine Bow River, and floated down to a boom at his sawmill.

Coe and Carter continued their domination of the Union Pacific business by suppressing private contractors and disgruntled employees who tried to cut, drive, and deliver ties on their own. Evidently, Coe and Carter had influential political connections in Washington. One particular incident provoked a complaint to the Department of the Interior in 1880. A "special agent" was dispatched to quell the wildcat operations, but in this case, a reciprocal complaint was made by the independents to the same department. An agreement was apparently reached by which Coe and Carter bought the forest lands they had logged for $1.23 an acre. Acreage on which they had operated for ten years was bought for $35,000 (Mullison 1909:50–51).

In 1884, Coe and Carter was dissolved. The senior member's son assumed control under the firm name of "Coe and Coe," which continued operations in the area (Mullison 1909:51). The Timber and Stone Act of 1878 was often used fraudulently by the timber interests to fell and remove timber on the public domain. Initially it was intended ". . . for building, agriculture, mining or other domestic purposes," since Wyoming Territory was considered a mineral district. The penalty for violating this statute was a $500 fine and up to six months imprisonment (U.S. Statutes at Large 1877–1879:88–89). Furthermore, it was customary for timber company employees to file on one hundred sixty acres if requested by the company, which would subsequently use the land for logging purposes. The dutiful employee was often rewarded with $100 (Mullison 1909:51). Coe and Coe continued operations on the Medicine Bow River and Rock Creek from 1880–1890. Mullison indicates that the amount of material driven and sold far exceeded the quantity they could have cut on their own holdings (Mullison 1909:53).

This decade (1880–1890) saw a substantial decrease in demand for ties due to internal problems within the Union Pacific Railroad. Only 1.2 million ties and 250,000 props were cut from the forest during that time (Mullison 1909:53).

In the spring of 1895, the Union Pacific cancelled all tie contracts, and Coe and Coe's dominance was on the wane, although they conducted operations after this date. The field was now open for a new company to control the tie industry (Mullison 1909:54).

The Carbon Timber Company

The cancelled tie contracts left a large number of unemployed timber men. Two enterprising businessmen from Hanna reasoned that eventually, the Union Pacific would require more ties. Butcher Charles L. Vagner and banker Louis R.

Meyer, offered to supply the lumbermen and provide the money for land entries under the Timber and Stone Act. In return, the men would cut ties and props, and prepare them for the 1896 drive in anticipation of the railroad's needs (Armstrong 1935:5).

This partnership cut ties and props from camps established on the Medicine Bow River and Rock Creek. In 1900, the company was incorporated as the successor to a partnership, capitalized at 1,000,000 dollars, chiefly in timberlands owned. The principal stockholders were the McGrews of Omaha (closely associated with the Union Pacific Railroad) and R. D. Meyer of Hanna. Mr. Meyer took over his father's interest in the company as a large stockholder. Andrew Olson was an employee of the company in the early days, and later became its president. As of 1914, R. D. Meyer was secretary and the younger McGrew was the general manager at Fort Steele (Potts 1914:1).

The company had a large operation at Fort Steele, including a box factory, sawmill, tie holding plant, main boom, and company store. A company town grew up around these facilities on the east bank of the river utilizing the company's 497 acres. They also had a sawmill plant, company store, and lumber camp near Encampment at Hog Park, and a sawmill and loading plant at Medicine Bow. They owned a total of 24,720 acres of timber land in 1914 (Potts 1914:3–4).

The Carbon Timber Company's prime years were from 1900 to 1906. Because of its close relationship with the Union Pacific Railroad, "it virtually controlled the Union Pacific's tie supply between Cheyenne and Ogden" (Potts 1914:3). It also manufactured wooden doors for coal and grain cars at Fort Steele for thirty-five cents each. In one year alone, sixty thousand doors were purchased by the Union Pacific, and because the Union Pacific Coal Company was closely associated with the railroad, all its orders for mine props were given to the Carbon Timber Company (Potts 1914:3–4).

Soon after formation of the Medicine Bow National Forest in 1902, timber cutting was regulated and government sales were initiated. This procedure became gradually more sophis-

Devils Gate Camp and Landing of the Carbon Timber Company.

Timber flume of the Carbon Timber Company on Devils Gate.

ticated and master plans were drawn up for cutting in various regions of the forest. When an area was ready to cut, a map, timber estimate, report, and stumpage appraisal were made. The appraisal determined a fair stumpage value for the sale. The sale was then advertised at this value for bidding. No bids were accepted below this value. The successful bidder made a contract with the Forest Service, which outlined the conditions of cutting and scaling, classes of timber to be manufactured, stumpage prices, and the plan of logging and brush disposal. An exact boundary was marked on the ground, and each tree was marked for cutting by Forest Service personnel. Actual logging practices were often monitored in the field by rangers (Medicine Bow Collection).

In 1906, the company negotiated two contracts with the forest, representing the first two large sales within the forest. The May 2 sale was located on the headwaters of Douglas Creek near Keystone, and involved 165 million measured board feet. The May 2 sale was ultimately cancelled in 1908 due to poor management by the company (Bruce 1959:68–69). It fared little better on the October 18 sale. Rangers Nelson and Gregg oversaw the sale, urging proper cleaning up practices.

The Carbon Timber Company requested and received a reduction in the number of board feet they were required to cut in the fall of 1907. During the spring drive of 1908, the water level was not favorable for driving, and a large amount of ties and mine props were left in the woods and along Douglas Creek. Thus, the company was paying the Forest Service for stumpage, but receiving nothing from the Union Pacific for undelivered ties. It was finally allowed to back out of the sale (Bruce 1959:71–72). The company was also involved in a timber trespass case on September 13, 1907, resulting from cutting beyond their rightful boundaries. A settlement of eighty thousand dollars was reached, half in cost and half in labor on a telephone line and wagon road (Medicine Bow Collection).

However, the Carbon Timber Company still had large operations in what would soon become the Hayden National Forest (Sierra Madres). It began operating on Encampment

Creek in 1902 with a large camp of almost five hundred men. By the following spring, the company had five hundred thousand ties ready to drive to the North Platte and Fort Steele (Blackhall 1915:1). About this time, it also took over the operations of J. C. Teller, who had cut from camps on Pass Creek, North and South Brush Creeks, and North French Creek from 1899 and 1902. He also delivered ties to the Union Pacific Railroad (Mullison 1909:55).

The *Grand Encampment Herald* regularly featured news of developments at Hog Park, as the town directly benefited from the logging operations. In 1902, the camp was described by a reporter for the papers:

> The tie camp headquarters occupies a very pretty spot in a park called Encampment Meadows, about twenty miles south of Grand Encampment, bordering on the Colorado state line.
>
> The establishment of the tie camp adds much to the development of the country. About three hundred men will be employed and most of them are men who have not previously resided in the vicinity of Grand Encampment. This will be a handsome addition to the population of southern Carbon Co. Grand Encampment will be the base of supplies for the tie camp, adding commercially to the interests of this place, and the new wagon road built to the camp opens up a new mining country which will also be tributary to Grand Encampment (*Grand Encampment Herald* 8/22/02).

The paper continued to praise the timber company and its contributions to the greater community until December 8, 1911, when it announced that the Hog Park tie camp would be abandoned the following spring after the tie drive. The paper stated that government regulations prevented the company from operating at a profit. "The present government policy is to let it stand for future generations or be consumed by forest fires, rather than let it be used to aid in the present prosperity and development of the country" (*Grand Encampment Herald*, 12/8/11).

The gradual decline of the Carbon Timber Company was brought about by a number of factors. It was easier to operate at a profit without any government controls or restrictions.

Furthermore, the company fell out of favor with the Union Pacific Railroad. It lost its preferred mine timber and car door business. Then in 1909 and 1910, a large number of ties was rejected by the railroad inspectors. The company had attempted to keep the price of ties at 65-66 cents apiece, but in 1910 Dan Wilt, a former company boss, attempted to deliver ties for a lower price by forming his own concern (the Standard Timber Company). As a result, by 1913 the Carbon Timber Company had almost no business from the Union Pacific. Wilt found that he could not deliver on his promise, but he had support from a Mr. Updike who was a personal friend of Mohler, the Union Pacific President. Although the Carbon Timber Company was able to mend its fences with the Union Pacific and receive part of its business that fall, it never again held a monopoly on the tie business (Potts 1914:2–8).

In 1915, the holdings of the Carbon Timber Company were sold at a sheriff's sale for $376,000. The Wyoming Timber Company was then formed, which dominated the logging industry until the 1950s (Medicine Bow Collection).

The End of an Era: Logging, 1915 to present

In 1913, the Union Pacific Railroad attempted to obtain its ties from sawed Douglas fir from the West Coast. However, the need was too great to be met by this source alone. As a result, Otto Gramm of Laramie received a contract, and subsequently organized the Foxpark Timber Company. Wilt's operation was also centered around Foxpark. Both men took advantage of the recently-constructed Laramie, Hahn's Peak and Pacific Railroad. Ties could be loaded and hauled by rail to Laramie, then treated at a special plant built there in 1902. As the railroad helped new companies get started in the southern portion of the Medicine Bow, the timber operations also saved the railroad from bankruptcy (Duthie 1916:4–6).

On January 7, 1914, the Forest Service offered a sale of all the timber adjacent to the railroad line from the Colorado state line to Foxpark. This sale was divided into blocks and sold over a period of years to different companies: Osea Nelson of the Union Timber Company, Dan Wilt of the Standard Timber Company, the Bergstrom Brothers of the Laramie Timber Company (Duthie 1916:4–5).

In 1915, the town of Gramm was built at the construction site of a large sawmill along the railroad line south of Foxpark. Most of the timber cutting operations at this time were located in this area, and rangers were shifted in the winter months from the northern stations to Foxpark. Duthie describes the workers and conditions at this time:

> A shortage of labor was at times a serious problem for the operators. Many of the tie cutters were 'floaters' recruited in Denver. In order to keep the men in camp in those days before radio and television, it was necessary to provide some amusement. Therefore, a poolhall was permitted to open in Gramm. Another already

Medicine Bow Collection — American Heritage Center
Skidding logs to a portable sawmill, Foxpark Timber Company Sale, February 1935.

existed at Foxpark. The men for the most part were a rugged lot and on several occasions the supervisor was faced with the problem of keeping bootleggers, gamblers, and other purveyors of illicit sport out of the camps. It took rugged men to buck ties in deep snow. There was a singular lack of labor-saving devices such as we exepct to find on similar operations today. For example, when the U.P. tie inspectors came to "load out" the ties, a crew of husky tie loaders worked in a rotating line. As the inspector marked each tie, which weighed from 150-250 pounds, a "loader" shouldered the tie and staggered up a ramp into the railroad car (Duthie 1916:5–6).

The Douglas Creek Tie Camp Company, located at Albany, was incorporated in 1917 under Hans Olson, Charles Engstrom, and Victor Strandquist for the January 5, 1917 timber sale on the main Medicine Bow. This company was actually a working subsidiary of the Wyoming Timber Company, which guaranteed its timber sales contracts. Some fifty-one thousand ties were cut from this sale (Medicine Bow Collection).

The year 1925 was one of the biggest logging years for the Medicine Bow National Forest. According to the *Rock River Review* (7/1/26), a record number of railroad ties, mine props, and lumber was cut. The major companies participating in this bonanza were the Wyoming Timber Company, Foxpark Timber Company, Stroup and Sheppard, and the Otto Lumber Company. The latter was organized by Otto Gramm (the founder of the Foxpark Timber Company), Andrew Olson (formerly of the Carbon Timber Company), and Hans and Ivor Olson (Andrew's brothers). Their first sale was in the Squaw and Lake Creek units north of Foxpark. However, they soon transferred operations to the Laramie River watershed in Colorado (Medicine Bow Collection).

Louis Coughlin, ranger and historian, states that 44,810,000 measured board feet of lumber were cut, with a value delivered at Laramie of $1,183,240 during the boom year of 1925. About five hundred men participated in the logging operations that year, and the Laramie tie treatment plant supported a working force of ninety-two men with a payroll of $139,520 (Medicine Bow Collection).

Headquarters of the Carbon Timber Company at Keystone.

The Wyoming Timber Company, headquartered in Hanna, was cutting in the forest in 1926 on Keystone and Horse Creeks with a large camp at Keystone (*Rawlins Reporter* 10/30/26). This camp was described by a local newspaper in April 1928:

> The logging camp of the Wyoming Timber Company at the Holmes, Wyoming post office, locally called Keystone, is an innovation as logging camps go in this part of Wyoming.
> It is located on Douglas Creek at the mouth of Keystone Creek. A sawmill also is located at the camp. A dozen buildings including the commissary, cookhouse, bunkhouse for the bachelors, two-room cabins for married men, and several barns, are scattered throughout the timber. Each cabin or barn and the sawmill as well, are equipped with electric lights. Kerosene lanterns and gasoline lamps have been banished from the camp. The tie hacks and lumber jacks from neighboring logging camps look with envy upon the Keystone camp and its "city lights" (Medicine Bow Collection).

The company was also cutting along Muddy Creek and had a camp known as "Camp No. 2" along this stream and another on Indian Creek (a small tributary). Ties cut in this area were driven down the tributaries to Douglas Creek, where a large boom was in place, and a dam built to flood the flats and pick up ties (*Laramie Republican-Boomering* 5/8/27).

The largest single timber sale to date on the Medicine Bow was awarded to the Wyoming Timber Company in 1934. It involved eighteen thousand acres on the Douglas Creek unit near Keystone and employed as many as two hundred men (Armstrong 1935:8).

The early 1920s saw a gradual change in the lumber industry with the development of a better road system in the forest and gasoline and diesel powered portable sawmills. With better roads, a portable unit could be hauled by tractor to a timber area, and ties could be sawed economically instead of hand-hewn. This development signaled the end of the tie hack tradition. One forest official was prophetic when he queried, "Is the time approaching when the picturesque tie hack with his broad ax will be replaced by a sawmill on wheels?" (Medicine Bow Collection).

Coughlin states that the first timber sale on the Medicine Bow Forest (Hayden Division) where motor vehicles were extensively used was in February 1924, with the firm of Daniels and Helmick. Stroud and Sheppard also used trucks to haul material from Dutton Creek to Rock River, a distance of twenty-five miles (Medicine Bow Collection).

In 1927, the cutting of telephone poles began on the forest. A treating plant for telephone poles was opened at Laramie in 1930 (Armstrong 1935:8).

The next step in the evolution of lumbering involved hauling logs to a permanent, fixed milling plant. With the steady improvement of roads and trucks, R. R. Crow and Company hauled logs from Barrett Creek to its mill in Saratoga in 1937 (Medicine Bow Collection).

During this period of transition, however, the tie hack was still very visible and the large tie drives continued. As late as 1938, the Wyoming Timber Company drove three hundred thousand ties down Douglas Creek to Fort Steele. Some three

A portable sawmill operation, R. R. Crow and Company Timber Sale, on the
Barrett Creek Unit (1937).

Employees of the Wyoming Timber Company break up a landing, preparing to
float ties down Douglas Creek from a timber sale on the Forest.

hundred and fifty thousand ties were driven down the Laramie River from northern Colorado to Laramie by the Foxpark Timber Company and the Otto Lumber Company. The latter drive was considered one of the largest in history *(Encampment Echo* 5/26/ 38).

An era ended in 1940 when the Union Pacific Railroad entirely discontinued the use of hand-hewn, river-driven ties (Medicine Bow Collection, Box 30). The last tie drive in the Medicine Bow was on Douglas Creek in the spring of that year.

In 1952, the Medicine Bow Forest advertised its third largest timber sale in history on the Rock Creek unit for eighty-three million measured board feet. Coughlin estimated that the cut would take ten years to complete, and a central processing plant would be constructed at Centennial. The principal products would be sawn railroad ties and finished lumber.

The value of the lumber industry to the surrounding communities can be measured in terms of dollars and cents from figures compiled by Coughlin. From 1902–1951, 842,111 measured board feet of lumber was obtained, valued at over two

Medicine Bow Collection — American Heritage Center
Pike poles are used to dismantle the landing for a tie drive on Douglas Creek.

Medicine Bow Collection — American Heritage Center

Breaking out a landing on Douglas Creek for the 1928 drive of the Wyoming Timber Company. Ties were stacked before the spring thaw awaiting sufficient water to carry them downstream to the North Platte River and Ft. Steele. Note that the drivers are using pickaroons to move the ties about.

million dollars. Twenty-five per cent of that amount had been distributed annually to all the counties in which the forest was located in lieu of taxes (Medicine Bow Collection). Ten per cent was retained by the Forest Service for road and trail maintenance. The balance was returned to the federal government (Armstrong 1935:31).

On December 10, 1951, the *Laramie Republican-Boomerang* reported the closing of the last of the great timber concerns, the Wyoming Timber Company. It had recently been working in the Keystone area and had been operating since about 1915 when it had absorbed the Carbon Timber Company.

VII.

THE LIFE OF THE TIE HACK

THE PROXIMITY of the Union Pacific Railroad and the large number of lodgepole pine reserves in the Medicine Bow Range made the business of supplying railroad ties the chief concern of the lumber interests from 1867 to 1940. The "tie hack" was the central figure in this industry. Initially, Civil War veterans and French Canadians were choppers; later in the century Swedes, Norwegians, Finns, Austrians, and Italians skilled in

Medicine Bow Collection — American Heritage Center
A typical tie hack's cabin on the West Beaver Foxpark Timber Company Sale; Ranger Williams is seated on the porch.

the use of a broadax predominated. (The broadax had a 10-12 inch blade, blunt on the opposite end.)

The ideal lodgepole pine was about eleven inches in diameter at breast height. An eight-foot length was standard, and in the 1870s the Union Pacific required a measurement of seven-by-seven inches. "Specifications demanded that the tie have at least five inches of hewn surface on both sides" (Linn 1973:20–21,31).

The process began by felling a suitable tree with a one-man bucksaw. The tie hack limbed the tree with a regular ax and measured his eight-foot length with a guide stick. He then "scored" the two opposite surfaces with an ax to reach proper thickness. This area was then hewn with the broadax. The remaining bark on top was removed with a "spud peeler," a long wooden handled tool with a curved blade on the end.

The hack used a one-man bucksaw to cut the tie to length.

Medicine Bow Collection — American Heritage Center
Tie hack "tools of the trade." From left to right: broadax, double-bladed ax, "spud peeler," 8-foot pole, pickaroon, one-man crosscut saw, and finished tie.

Medicine Bow Collection — American Heritage Center
A suitable lodgepole pine is being sawed by a tie hack using a one-man buck saw.

The last step involved removing the bark from the underside of the tie not exposed during the earlier operations. It was usually the practice to hew the entire tree before cutting it to eight-foot lengths. A "pickaroon" was used to move the tie about. This tool resembled an ax with a metal point on one end.

Joan Drego Pinkerton, author of *Knights of the Broadax* (1981:19), states: "A good hack worth his salt could cut fifty ties a day . . .", although twenty to twenty-five was probably closer to the average. During the rush to complete the first transcontinental railroad, the hack received thirty-five to sixty cents per tie. This price dropped after the railroad was completed (Homsher 1949:58). Coe and Carter paid as little as seven to eight cents per tie before the turn of the century (Interview with Louis Sederlin by Ranger Bruce Torgny 2/20/35). A local newspaper, reporting on a successful strike of the Foxpark Tie and Timber Workers Union in 1934, stated that they were to receive twenty-five cents for a first-grade tie,

Medicine Bow Collection — American Heritage Center
After felling the tree, the tie hack clears it of limbs, preparing it for hewing.

Medicine Bow Collection — American Heritage Center
With an 8 foot pole, the tie hack measures off the length of a tie, as specified by
the Union Pacific.

Medicine Bow Collection — American Heritage Center
The tie hack scores two surfaces with a double-bladed ax to proper thickness for
hewing with a broad ax.

A tie hack hewing a tie with his broadax. The surface has already been "scored" with an ax to aid in hewing.

Tie hack peeling the bark from the tie with a "spud peeler." Hewing has been completed, and the hack will soon cut the tie to length. Finally, he will peel the bark from the underside.

The bark is peeled off the underside of the tie with a spud peeler.

By using a pickaroon, the tie hack is able to skid the tie along the ground to the skid road, where it will be piled for hauling.

seventeen cents for seconds, and twelve cents apiece for thirds (Medicine Bow Collection). In 1904, the Carbon Timber Company was paying twelve to fourteen cents per tie (*Grand Encampment Herald*, 7/1/40). The price could then fluctuate significantly, depending on the company and time period, but it did not appear that a tie hack would ever get rich.

Cutting could take place winter and summer. The ties were easiest to haul with snow cover. However, on a government sale, stumps could not be more than twelve inches high. Therefore, winter work might involve shoveling four feet to five feet of snow from around the base of the tree to be felled. Horse teams were used to sled the loaded ties out to tie landings along "drivable" streams. Ties were carefully stacked in close proximity to the stream awaiting the spring thaw and high water. "Splash" dams were often built near the headwaters of smaller streams to raise the level of the stream adjacent to the tie landings and to flood low flat areas.

Landings were then broken with pike poles and picaroons, and ties dumped into the water ready for driving. If a splash dam was in place, it would be opened to allow the logs to "surge" down the channel, riding the crest. A gang of drivers still had to follow the ties and keep them moving. Occasionally, jams would become so severe that dynamite was needed to jar them loose. Frequently used drive streams were periodically cleaned to remove obstacles such as deadfalls and large rocks.

On the west side of the Medicine Bows and in the Sierra Madres, ties were driven down tributary channels to the North Platte and northward to Fort Steele where they were caught by a large boom. A continuous chain hauled them from the river and past tie inspectors for grading. They were loaded finally into railway cars. The same general practice was followed in drives on the east side of the Snowy Range.

The tie industry, then, required rugged men who could fell a tree, hew a railroad tie, and wrestle it down a freezing mountain torrent. Some were drowned in the tie drives, and others received severe fractures and other injuries. The danger of forest fires was ever present. Camps were isolated, and the

A drive of ties and saw logs jammed on Douglas Creek. Tie drivers sometimes had to resort to the use of dynamite to dislodge the material.

Bull chain and boom at Ft. Steele. The boom caught the river driven ties, and the bull chain pulled them up and along the ramp past Union Pacific tie inspectors. The approved ties were loaded directly onto waiting railroad cars.

tie hack and his family were far from medical help in any emergency. An influenza epidemic hit the Wyoming Timber Company camp complex at French Creek during the winter of 1918–1919. Out of forty-six camp residents in four adjacent camps, thirty-six were taken ill and nine died. Rangers Cyril Webster and Edwin Bunnell cared for the sick, and somehow avoided being stricken.

The era of the tie hack appears romantic and adventurous with the passage of time, but the reality involved hardships and toil that few experience in the 1980s.

VIII.

FIRE PREVENTION

IN 1912, Forest Supervisor C. M. Granger prepared a comprehensive fire prevention plan. Granger described the Medicine Bows as being very adaptable to a system of lookout points, likening the forest geographically to a semi-flattened cone spreading out from a sharply rising peak (Medicine Bow Peak) in the center. The forest could be effectively viewed from three types of lookouts: 1) primary lookouts commanding views of large areas, which were manned throughout the fire season and were connected by telephone to ranger headquarters and the supervisor's office; 2) secondary lookouts located on less

Medicine Bow Collection — American Heritage Center
Ranger E. J. Williams and helpers haul map board, linoleum and supplies up Medicine Bow peak to the fire lookout.

prominent points with towers, which were visited each day during the fire season, and also had telephone connections; and 3) tertiary lookouts which had neither towers nor telephones and were visited by rangers only during danger periods. As of 1912, the Medicine Bows had one primary, four secondary, and numerous tertiary lookouts (Medicine Bow Collection).

The primary lookout was established on Medicine Bow Peak at 12,005 feet in 1909, due to the persistence of P. S. Lovejoy. From that peak and two others nearby, eighty percent of the forest could be viewed. Fred Miller, the first lookout on the forest, resided in a log shack he built himself on Lookout Lake, 1,500 feet below the peak. Every day, between July 1 and September 15, Miller would begin the climb to the top of the peak, where he surveyed the forests using nine-power binoculars, a map of the forest, and a compass. Miller also constructed a small rock shelter on the peak itself. Granger described Miller as "absolutely dependable and faithful to his trust, for on his vigilence depends the safety of millions of

Medicine Bow Collection — American Heritage Center

Lookout's cabin at Lookout Lake. Fred J. Miller, first Medicine Bow Peak fire lookout (1909) displays his handiwork. Miller also built a stone shelter atop Medicine Bow Peak. He climbed the mountain every morning from Lookout Lake to search for fires.

Medicine Bow Collection — American Heritage Center
MEDICINE BOW PEAK LOOKOUT
An improvement over Fred Miller's accommodations (left), the lookout
could stay on the summit on a 24-hour basis.

dollars worth of public property . . ." Miller also fulfilled the qualifications of unusual good health and the ability to live alone. "Nothing short of a broken leg would keep him off the peak when he should be there" (Medicine Bow Collection).

In 1921, the Medicine Bow National Forest made news by hiring Wyoming's first female fire lookout. Miss Lorraine Lindaley was stationed on Medicine Bow Peak, and lived in the ten-by-twelve-foot one-room cabin at the base of the peak (Armstrong 1935:25). Women were again employed during World War II due to manpower shortage; Medicine Bow had five female lookouts during the summer of 1944 (*Laramie Republican-Boomerang* 7/27/44).

Notable fires included the South French Creek burn in June

Medicine Bow Collection — American Heritage Center
Rangers toil up Medicine Bow Peak under the weight of telephone poles for construction of a phone line to the peak.

Medicine Bow Collection — American Heritage Center
Lorraine Lindaley (1921) was the first female fire lookout in the Medicine Bows.

1930. Seeding was proposed but natural reproduction was successful (Medicine Bow Collection). In 1931, the Toltec fire in LaBonte Canyon in the Laramie Peak area burned about one thousand acres (Medicine Bow Collection).

During the 1930s and early 1940s, Civilian Conservation Corps (CCC) camps were instrumental in constructing lookout towers as well as fighting fires. By 1935, there were six lookouts on the main Medicine Bow, and two on the Hayden (Armstrong 1935:24). By 1937, there were six "fire danger stations" established: Sandstone Ranger Station, Somber Hill, Encampment, Mullen Creek, Ryan Park, and Esterbrook (Medicine Bow Collection). In addition to the aforementioned, there have been lookouts at some point in time on Jelm Mountain, Spruce Mountain, Kennaday Peak, Blackhall Mountain, Bridger Peak, Fletcher Peak, Esterbrook, and at Long Lake.

Medicine Bow Collection — American Heritage Center
Although the forest began a comprehensive fire prevention program in 1912, some fires were inevitable. Here, firefighters battle the devastating Turpin Creek blaze in 1915.

IX.

PICK AND SHOVEL: THE MINING INDUSTRY

THE PRESENCE OF precious metals in the Medicine Bow Mountains had been suspected quite early. Several accounts state that Captain Douglas, a member of Sir George Gore's hunting expedition, found gold in the Medicine Bow Mountains in 1856 and that Douglas Creek was named for him (Medicine Bow Collection). F. V. Hayden of the U.S. Geological Survey stated that "valuable specimens of ores and placer gold" were brought to him from the mountains southwest of Fort Steele (Beeler 1906:11).

Medicine Bow Collection — American Heritage Center

HOLMES MINING CAMP
The buildings have been removed, and the site is now the Holmes Campground.

John H. Mullison, an early ranger on the Medicine Bow
Forest and a pioneer in the area, wrote an interesting account
of early mining evidence in Mullison Park. In the Forest Atlas
for 1909, Mullison described early shafts and signs of mining
on Upper Brush Creek that had been pointed out to him in
1870 by Ute Indians. In 1886, he investigated by sinking a
shaft "in one of the old depressions." Mullison claimed workers
broke through into a shaft that had been sunk at some earlier
date and found an elk's ivory with a human face carved upon
it. These depressions and workings reportedly extended for
more than a half mile (Mullison 1909:29–32).

In the same area, a small creek had been worked with
evidence of a stone retaining wall and five different excavations
along the stream. Trees that were over one hundred seventy-five
years old in 1870 were found growing out of the debris from
a shaft near this location (Mullison 1909:32).

Gold on Douglas Creek

The Douglas Creek District was formed as a result of the
discovery of gold by Iram Moore in the fall of 1868 in stream
gravels on a tributary of Douglas Creek. This area later became
known as Moore's Gulch and was the first well documented
gold discovery in the Medicine Bow Mountains.

Miners rushed to the area. Using such rudimentary methods
as gold panning, sluice boxes, and rockers, they extracted an
estimated $8,000 worth of gold in the spring of 1869. Many
of the washings yielded $2 to 2.50 to the pan. According to
Beeler, "nuggets have been weighed from 16 to 68 pennyweight
each, (one pennyweight is equal to 1/20th of an ounce) but
the majority of the gold is in shape of finer particles varying
from the fine or flour gold up to flat nuggets an eighth of a
inch long" (Beeler 1906:17). Although the principal mineral
value was in gold, copper and platinum were also present.
Knight estimated that $229,000 (12,040 ounces) was produced
in the Douglas Creek District by 1893. The district along
Douglas Creek and its tributaries is 15 miles long and 10 miles

wide. Gold bearing gravels ranged from 3-20 feet in thickness. The best concentrations were found where the gravels and bedrock made contact (Hausel 1980:22).

Traditionally, the second phase in mining an area is tracing the sources of gold found in placer deposits. Because much of the placer gold was coarse and had pieces of quartz adhering to it, it was reasoned that it had not traveled any great distance from the source (Hausel 1980:25). As a result, lode mines were soon discovered in quartz veins with secondary values in copper. The principal mines were the Keystone, New Rambler, Douglas, and the Florence.

The Douglas Mine

Located on the west bank of Douglas Creek, the mine was discovered in 1870. A seven foot wide ore body was found at a depth of thirty-five feet as well as three smaller veins at deeper levels, all containing copper in chalcopyrite, chalcocite, and some gold. Currey (1965:8) states that "almost all traces of the mine were obliterated when the present road was constructed along the west bank of upper Douglas Creek."

The Keystone Mine

According to H. C. Beeler (1906:47), this was one of the early mines in the district. This vein consisted of "free gold" and gold in association with pyrite and pyrrhotite. In 1890, a twenty-stamp mill was constructed on the property. Operations ceased in 1893. The total production was estimated at $96,000 (Osterwald et al. 1966:66). "The mine plant was dismantled and the shaft sealed in the 1950s" (Currey 1965:9).

The Florence Mine

This property was described as one of the oldest in the district. Currey states that operations ceased in 1889 and that the machinery was moved to the Keystone Mine (Currey 1965:9). Gold was found in small pockets, but it was in small and discontinous quantities. Beeler gave a total production figure of $50,000 in 1906.

Keystone mining community in 1906; forest fires and indiscriminate cutting have taken their toll on the slopes above the mining camp.

A twenty-stamp mill was constructed in 1890 at Keystone to process gold. The mine and mill were demolished and the shafts sealed over in 1950s.

The New Rambler Mine

The mine was first opened for gold, then emphasis shifted to copper in 1900. It was owned by the Rambler Mining and Smelting Company. Production figures in 1906 showed that 1,928 dry tons of ore were shipped, averaging 19 percent copper valued at $77,622. A "matte" smelter was constructed on the property capable of handling 40 tons per day (Beeler 1906:42). In August 1918, the mine buildings were destroyed by fire and mining ceased (Hess 1926:134–35; McCallum and Orback 1968:9). The New Rambler was probably the only property in the region actually to market any platinum.

The Gold Hill Boom

This district was established in 1890. According to Louis E. Coughlin, the first strike was made in 1888 by Benjamin W. Arundell, who later served as a ranger on the Hayden

Medicine Bow Collection — American Heritage Center   *Photo by H. C. Hilton*
The Little Florence Claim near the Keystone mining district, 1925.

Medicine Bow Collection — American Heritage Center
Many Scandinavians came to the Medicine Bows as tie hacks, but Soren Sorenson prospected for gold in the Rambler mines.

Forest. He could not get financial backing until the fall of 1890 when a general rush began. Laramie, Saratoga, Carbon, and Arlington all began to construct wagon roads into the area. The Saratoga road, having the shortest distance to traverse, arrived first. Col. Stephen W. Downey of Laramie built a stamp mill at Gold Hill which was in operation in 1897 (*Rawlins Republican* 8/19/26), but it was described as doing "very poor work." That same year the Fairview Mine, discovered by Joe Lucin on Brush Creek, was described as the premier mine in the district with one assay showing a $364/ton. *The Saratoga Sun* (2/4/92) described winter at the Gold Hill Camp:

> It has been no easy matter to keep Gold Hill from being snowed under this winter. Accurate records have been kept, and these show that snow fall has totalled 329½ inches or more than 27 feet in four months.

The Acme Consolidated Gold and Copper Mining Company of Laramie and Boston, Massachuetts, had twenty claims at

Courtesy American Heritage Center
The mill at Gold Hill in 1900. The Gold Hill mining district was established in 1890 and flourished until around 1905. The area experienced a brief rebirth in 1931.

Gold Hill which it had begun working in 1900. By 1905, grandiose plans were laid for a townsite with twenty-five cottages, a hotel, and power plant for electricity (*Centennial Post* 10/30/05). A great deal of money was spent in development work equipping the mines with steam operated hoists utilizing large boilers. The Laramie, Hahns Peak, and Pacific Railroad was to be extended to Gold Hill. Boston interests under Isaac Van Horn probably kept the camp alive with their financial backing long after it should have died a natural death.

It was reported in 1897 that a rich vein had been cut in one of the company's properties and that plans were underway for constructing a stamp mill (*Rawlins Republican* 9/29/31). In 1893 it was estimated that $3,000 (145 ounces) of gold had been produced in the district (Knight 1893). The Acme shaft reached a depth of 169 feet in 1905 when the public interest reached its peak.

The railroad was never built to the camp and interest in Gold Hill soon lagged, only to be rekindled in 1931. R. M. "Scotty" Levon found a vein of free milling gold (the Camp Bird) on the Magnolia claim which had been prospected in the early days of the district. Levon was backed by F. E. Anderson, a prominent Laramie attorney. Plans were underway to install a mill at the mine site. However, as in the past, reports were greatly exaggerated, and Gold Hill once again sank into obscurity. The following article is interesting as it describes the condition of the old mining camp in 1931:

> There are twenty-five or thirty cabins standing as reminders of the beginning of what might have been a thriving mining settlement. Snow has caved in the roof of the old hotel building, but the post office, two saloon buildings and other souvenirs of bygone days are still standing (*Laramie Republican-Boomerang* 3/21/31).

In 1931, Otto L. Burns, a prospector from Gold Hill in 1891, was interviewed by Ernest Linford and related that in its heyday, there were about five hundred people at Gold Hill, with four saloons, several groceries and hotels. He also mentioned the Leviathon and Little Giant as early claims at Gold Hill (Medicine Bow Collection).

Cooper Hill Prospects

Rich float and an outcrop of galena were found in 1888, and the Cooper Hill District was formed shortly thereafter. Principal values were in gold, lead, copper, and silver carried in quartz veins. H. C. Beeler claims that this district encompassed part of the "Old Herman Mining District." Camp Herman was represented by a set of "ruined cabins" near Sand Lake, according to Louis Coughlin's 1951 recollections. The Cooper Hill Deep Mining Company had the Little Johnnie and Laura Bell claims on Bald Mountain in the Herman District. The company was capitalized at $1 million. The trustees included Thomas C. Van Bentusen, Alexander B. Hamilton, Dwight Smith and Thomas Simpson.

A ten-stamp mill was constructed in 1898, and although hundreds of tons of ore were processed, recovery was poor. The principal mines were the Albion and the Emma G. Others in the area included the Charlie, Silver King, Cooper Hill, and Richmond Mines. The Rip Van Winkle Consolidated Company was still doing work in the area as late as 1906. One source states that no ore was ever marketed and no production figures have been found. Most of the mining locations at Cooper Hill are just outside the forest boundary or on patented mining claims (Beeler 1906:59–60; Hausel 1980:39–43).

Centennial Ridge Mines

The discovery of gold deposits in stream gravels on Centennial Ridge led to significant lode discoveries in 1875–1876. The district was established as a result of this activity in 1876. Accounts vary on the actual discovery of gold and the Centennial Mine. The *Centennial Post* (1908 and 1909) carried a story on the mine's discovery, relating how a group of hunters crossing the mountains stopped to rest and found gold glimmering among the rocks. They picked up samples and showed them to Col. Stephen Downey of Laramie. The samples were tested and "pronounced to be gold, pure gold" (Weigand 1976:4). The Centennial Mine was the chief producer of the district. The ore was described as "free-milling gold associated with quartz veins" (Hausel 1980:32) and averaged 1.5 ounces per ton. The mine's total production was placed at $90,000 (4,780 ounces) of gold (McCallum 1968:10). An ore sample from the mine won first prize at the Paris Exposition in 1876. The vein was traced until a fault was encountered and never relocated (Hausel 1968:10). Stephen W. Downey was the president of the Centennial Gold Mining Company and I. P. Lambing was the superintendent at the mine. A ten-stamp mill was built at the base of the mountain and connected to the mine by means of a 425-foot tramway (Weigand 1976:10).

The Utopia and the Free Gold were the only other mines with documented ore production in the district.

After 1900, the district experienced new excitement when platinum and palladium were extracted from copper ores in the New Rambler mine near Holmes, several miles to the southwest. This precipitated new mining activity in the region. A number of new mines were developed on Centennial Ridge.

In 1896, Jacob Schnitzler discovered a copper claim on the west side of Centennial Ridge. He dug two tunnels, one of which exposed "a small mass of sulphides or arsenides, probably less than a foot in diameter, . . . where a small fracture crosses the tunnel at right angles. The mineral having been determined as simply pyrite, little more attention was paid to it, and the tunnel continued seventy feet" (Hess 1926:130).

However, in 1923 the ore from this tunnel was assayed and found to contain platinum. A rush ensued to stake out properties in the vicinity during the winter while the ground was still covered with snow.

Exaggerated claims appeared in the press that attracted nationwide attention. Frank L. Hess and Charles W. Henderson of the U.S. Geological Survey visited the district in June 1924 "to examine the new prospects" as commerical platinum deposits were considered rare. Their analysis was not promising. Hess concluded his 1924 report (published in 1926) with the following statement about the district's potential:

> Platinum metals, in very small quantities, are undoubtedly present on Centennial Ridge. At some places there may be larger masses of rich ore than the small pockets found in the Middle Schnitzler Tunnel, but the writer believes the chances for such discoveries are too few to warrant the expenditures of money, time and labor (Hess 1926:135).

Unfortunately no one was listening. A local promoter, A. J. Hull, was the prime mover in advertising the potential of the area and even laid out a townsite known as "Platinum City" along the right-of-way of the Laramie, Hahn's Peak, and Pacific Railroad, about two miles south of Centennial. The Wyoming Platinum and Gold Mining Syndicate sold stocks to the public based on a number of claims Hull and Schnitzler were working. The *Laramie Leader* (4/8/31) carried a story on Platinum City showing photographs of the townsite, power plant, mill, and refinery. Apparently A. J. Hull had processed a half ton of ore worth over $22,000 in April 1931. The article continues:

> For some time a city has been platted adjoining the mining property, ahd when Mr. Hull has the mines sufficiently developed to need a small army of men, the lots will be sold, houses and stores built, and a model city started, with everything that goes to make a model city according to the best plans *(Laramie Leader* 4/8/31).

Regardless of A. J. Hull's sincerity, by 1934 he was indicted for mail fraud. The Wyoming Platinum and Gold Mining Syndicate had disposed of over five hundred thousand shares of stock, mostly out of state, and had distributed circulars and letters which apparently exaggerated the claims that the syndicate owned. Hull was never convicted and continued to prospect and work in the Centennial area for many years.

Copper in the Sierra Madres: The Encampment District

Although Ed Haggarty did not make the famous Rudefeha copper strike until 1897, prospecting had been carried on since the close of the Civil War (and perhaps earlier) in the Sierra Madre Mountains. In 1864, J. W. Southwick noticed quartz veins running along the surface on what later became the Kurtze Chatterton Mine on Copper Creek, but did not develop the property. Boney Ernest and Tom Sun located four claims in 1872 on this property, and Bill Savage took up a fifth claim nearby in 1874. In 1876, these claims were officially surveyed and application was made for patent. However, the parties abandoned their claims and Kurtze Chatterton purchased them several years later (Spencer 1904:12).

In 1874, a man named Harper found copper-bearing float on what bacame the Doane-Rambler mine at Rambler. He sunk a ten-foot hole, but soon abandoned the property. In 1881, George Doane and associates took up the claim and did considerable development work, sinking a shaft to a depth of seventy-five feet. This effort represented "the first systematic mining in the district" (Spencer 1904:12) and the earliest mining for copper ores. One source stated that Doane found previous evidence of mining on this claim and two cabins with loopholes cut in the walls for defense. This probably pre-dated Harper's work and suggests early, although undocumented, mining in the Sierra Madres (Kennedy 1925:69–72).

The Bridger mine was located in 1876 on the Continental Divide. Frank O. Williams discovered silver-lead deposits, with traces of gold. Williams also discovered the Charter Oak mine which later became one of the better mines in the district (Spencer 1904:13).

No other significant discoveries were made in the district until 1896 when Al Huston and Ben Cullerton discovered free gold in Purgatory Gulch (Spencer 1904:13). This strike spurred outside interest which would soon switch to copper.

The Rudefeha or Ferris-Haggarty Mine

This great copper mine was the premier development in the district, and with it rose and fell the fortunes of the Encampment region. It was discovered by Ed Haggarty who had been grubstaked by George Ferris, Robert Deal, and John Rumsey. Haggarty actually discovered the lode on June 20, 1897, but did not stake out a claim at that time due to snow cover. He returned on July 25:

> Haggarty at once set up the location stake, erected a monument, and thus took possession, by law, of a twenty-acre tract of mining land, which he christened in his location notice as the "Rudefeha" lode mining claim the name being composed of the two first letters of the name of each of the partners — Rumsey, Deal, Ferris and Haggarty (Coutant 1947:120)

Rumsey's interest was soon bought out by Ferris. In the spring and summer of 1898, Haggarty and party worked the claim and staked out others nearby. A wagon road was cut into the area, a more permanent camp set up and development begun in earnest (Coutant 1947:120–121).

By October 1898, the first load of ore was hauled out to Fort Steele and the railroad. The first railroad car of ore was sent to the Chicago Copper Refining Company and was found to contain 33.18 percent copper valued at $6,664 (Junge 1972:8).

In 1899, Ed Haggarty sold his interest in the proprty for $30,000 and returned to his native England. George Ferris was killed in a wagon accident in the Sierra Madres. However, the Ferris-Haggarty Copper Mining Company had been formed by Willis George Emerson and Barnard McCaffery in January 1899, and continued to operate after the departure of Ferris and Haggarty. Emerson was a great promoter and was partially responsible for the rush to the Encampment District. He had an office in Denver to advertise the mine and actually laid out the official Encampment townsite, although structures had already been built on the site in a haphazard manner (Junge 1972:9–10). The mine was developed in a systematic manner.

By 1902, a smelter had been built near Encampment on the west bank of the Encampment River to process the ore. A four mile wooden pipeline was built from a reservoir on the South Fork of the Encampment River (south of town) to supply water to the smelter. A converter was added to the plant facility in 1903, so that 90 percent pure copper ingots could be produced, thus saving on transportation costs (Beeler 1905:10–11; Junge 1972:11).

Transportation of the ore from mine to mill was streamlined by means of a sixteen-mile aerial tramway, an engineering feat for its time. One can imagine the logistical difficulties involved in constructing 304 wooden support towers and stringing cable across mountainous terrain over the Continental Divide. Buckets capable of holding 700 pounds of ore each and moving at an average speed of four miles per hour were suspended from the cables. At full production, the tramway could deliver 984 tons of ore per day. Three auxillary power stations were built at intervals along the route, and all construction was accomplished in seven months (Beeler 1905:10).

Mining Camps in The Encampment District

Duane Smith, in his fine study, *Rocky Mountain Mining Camps* (1967), discusses a unique feature of the mining frontier urbanization:

> For centuries the frontier had been the home of the individualist, where men and women lived their lives in a basically rural envoironment. By choice or adaptation these people had become the cutting edge of civilization; behind their line of advance grew the refinements of rural life and the first signs of urban existence. In contrast, on the mining frontier the camp — the germ of a city — appeared almost simultaneously with the opening of the region. Individual prospectors or prospecting parties conducted the initial exploration, but their success quickly attracted others who formed the basis for the nascent community.
>
> The urban nature of the movements increased the speed and direction of development. Within weeks or months, the refinements of civilization appeared to the frontiersman. By visiting the

camp, anyone with enough money could secure favors and pleasures which had been denied to earlier frontiers for as long as a generation. Also available were newspapers, recent periodicals, the latest fashions, and new equipment of all types which, together with other similar items, gave the frontier an up-to-date and progressive character. To be sure, this facade could disappear as quickly as it had come, but in the participant and the observer it produced a different reaction to the frontier than would have occurred otherwise (Smith 1967:4–5).

A number of settlements or camps developed as a result of the mining activity in the Encampment district. Elwood was considered a transfer point for supplies, mail, and passengers traveling west to the Ferris-Haggarty Mine from Encampment. During the winter months, it was necessary to transfer from wagon or stage to sleds. Elwood was located about six miles northwest of Encampment on Tennant Creek and was named after Tom Elwood, stage driver. At the height of the copper boom, the population of Elwood approached one hundred, and a post office was located there (Junge 1972:13).

The next settlement west was known as Battle, named for the Fraeb fight in 1841. The site was laid out in 1898 and contained forty structures, including four general stores, five saloons, livery stables, two hotels, a post offce and a newspaper called *The Battle Miner*. The town acted as a supply point for area mines, and a stopover for stage and freight traffic. The two story Hotel de Maine was probably the dominant structure in Battle and was built from sawed lumber instead of logs (Armstong 1935:17).

Passengers traveled from Walcott by stage in six-horse Concords. The distance was 24 miles to Saratoga and 44 miles to Encampment. In 1905, daily stages left Encampment for Battle, a distance of 12 miles, Dillon 19 miles, and Copperton 20 miles (Beeler 1905:5). Battle is little more than a site today, as the Civilian Conservation Corps destroyed the crumbling buildings in the 1930s. A few log cabins still stand and appear to be used as summer homes.

The small town of Rambler grew up around the Doane-Rambler Mine on the west side of the Continental Divide about 1.5 miles west of Battle. Located along a north-south drainage in a meadow north of Battle Lake, the town was used as a stopping place for those en route to the Ferris-Haggarty mine. It also had a post office. The Rambler camp appears to be the earliest settlement in the district, as the Doane-Rambler was the earliest operating mine.

Copperton was named for the related mining efforts in the area. It was used as a supply point and post office for cattle and sheep operations in the area. It was strategically located near the confluence of Haggarty and Little Sandstone creeks where the road leading to the Ferris-Haggarty Mine diverged.

The camp of Dillon grew up along this branch, one mile before reaching the Ferris-Haggarty Mine. One explanation for its existence was that saloons were barred from Rudefeha in

Courtesy American Heritage Center
The mining town of Battle in the Sierra Madres was established in 1898 and boasted 40 buildings and a newspaper. The decaying structures were razed by the CCC in the 1930s.

1902. However, Beeler's 1905 description indicates that more was involved in its development:

> The town of Dillon has an altitude of 9,000 feet, is three-quarters of a mile southwest of the Ferris-Haggarty mine and is the principal supply point of this section. Supply houses, hotel accommodations, livery barn, etc., are located here and a good trade is carried on (Beeler 1905: 18).

Dillon was named for Malachi W. Dillon, who owned a boardinghouse in the town. Perhaps the most important feature of the camp was the newspaper, *The Dillon Doublejack,* edited and written by Grant Jones. Because Jones had previously worked for large newspapers in Chicago, he was able to disseminate information about the mining district over a wide area to "the outside world." Jones had 392 annual subscribers before going to press in December 1902 and advertised:

> We need postage stamps, express money orders, drafts and checks. For two dollars of any of these we will send the Doublejack for twelve months to anybody anywhere. (*Rawlins Daily Times:* from *Dillon Doublejack* Vol. 1, No. 1-12/20/02).

Sadly, Jones died the following June in a bizarre incident involving the injection of morphine by his cabin mate while Jones was intoxicated.

The end of the line was reached at Rudefeha, one mile northeast of Dillon. A sizable community grew up around the tremendous workings at the Ferris-Haggarty. In 1903, one hundred twenty-five men were employed, and in its peak year, 1904, two hundred men were on the payroll (Beeler 1905: 17; Junge 1972: 18).

Waning Days of the Ferris-Haggarty Mine

Originally, a 250 foot shaft with two levels had produced most of the ore at the Ferris-Haggarty Mine. A tunnel was run 390 feet below the shaft opening along the creek, which connected with the shaft, and a 180 foot winze with drifts was dug. The width of the ore vein averaged about 20 feet and the ore averaged about six to eight percent copper. The entire mining operation was very efficient:

> The ore is stoped out by machine drills, thrown into shoots [sic], cropped to the tunnel level and hauled out by compressed air haulage, seven cars to a train, whence it is dumped directly into tramway ore bins and shipped over the tramway to the smelter (Beeler 1905:17).

The Ferris-Haggarty went through many different ownerships. It was purchased by the North American Copper Company in the fall of 1902 for one million dollars. From 1898 to 1904, the mine produced $1,400,000 in copper, qualifying it as a legitimate large-scale mine. By December 23, 1904, the Penn-Wyoming Copper Company succeeded North American, but the economic base of the latter had apparently been shaky, and the financial practices of the new owner were questionable. Additionally, the operation had always suffered due to the distance from the railroad. As a result, the Saratoga and Encampment Railroad was built from Walcott but did not reach Encampment until July 18, 1908. The railroad had been an expensive project under the Penn-Wyoming Company, and had arrived too late to save the operation (Junge 1972:19–21).

Ownership changed hands once again in February 1909, when the Penn-Wyoming Company sold out to United Smelters, Railway and Copper Company. By the fall of 1910, the new company went into bankruptcy. The properties went into litigation until foreclosure proceedings took place in 1913. The properties were stripped of their equipment. The demise of the mine that had always been the dominant property in the Encampment district naturally brought about the downfall of the whole region. The smaller mining communities declined and became ghost towns while other copper properties languished.

Failure of the Ferris-Haggarty can be traced to poor financial management and disastrous fires in March 1906 and May 1907 that destroyed the concentrating mill, power house, boiler room and smelter, all of which had to be rebuilt at great expense because they were under-insured. Perhaps a more important cause was the wild fluctuations and speculation in the national copper market during those years. In 1902, copper prices fell but rose the following year and continued to do so until a decline in 1908, which did not trend upward until 1912. Large sums of money had been spent in developing the mine with a tramway, smelter and concentrator. The absence of a railroad until late 1908 kept transportation costs high. Finally, the mine had limited copper reserves in comparison to some of the really large operations in Montana and Michigan.

With the decline of the copper industry, the area returned to ranching and pastoral pursuits. The communities of Encampment and Saratoga endured, and today attract tourists to the area for fishing, hunting, and general recreation.

Mining Around Laramie Peak

The core of the North Laramie Mountains is composed of coarse-grained granites of the Precambrian age. Laramie Peak is the dominant topographic feature rising to 10,272 feet, approximately 1,000 feet higher than the next highest peaks. The range is rugged with narrow ridges and broad gullies, and valleys with steep gradients (Segerstrom and Weisner 1977:B2; Spencer 1916:52).

Although the region has experienced prospecting for mineral deposits throughout recent history, none of the efforts was particularly profitable. According to Arthur C. Spencer:

> Evidences of prospecting, assigned by local tradition to the period immediately following the discovery of gold in the Cherry Creek and Pikes Peak districts in Colorado, are to be noted from place to place within the area of crystalline rocks lying northwest to Laramie Peak. Stories of gold having been won by individuals and of lost mines are current, but no printed records are known to justify the belief that there has ever been any production worthy of mention (Spencer 1916:56).

A pocket of gold ore was discovered in the 1890s near Warbonnet Peak which caused increased but short-lived activity near the head of LaPrele and LaBonte Creeks. Nothing resulted from these efforts. General prospecting began around 1875, and continued with a concentration on copper ores after 1900 (Spencer 1916:56–57).

The Esterbrook mine is located just south of the Esterbrook townsite on the Douglas claim and was first developed by the Boston-Wyoming Copper Company with hoists and boilers. It was the most extensively developed mine in the region. It was studied by Henry L. Beeler, state geologist, in 1902 during its early exploratory phase (indicating a discovery date shortly before that time.) In 1902, fifty tons of ore were mined with an average value of $15/ton. Additionally, 35,588 pounds of hand-sorted ore contained 1.3 ounces of silver/ton, and .03502 ounces of gold/ton (Spencer 1916:63–64). Other lesser developments were the Three Cripples, Maggie Murphy, and Big Five, none of which had any significant production.

The Warbonnet District is comprised of mining locations near the head of LaBonte Canyon and Warbonnet Peak. Efforts in this district were directed toward the extraction of copper ores. The major developments consisted of the Pyramid Mine, the Copper King, and the Oriole.

X.

THE SHEPHERD AND THE COWBOY

THE GRAZING POTENTIAL of the Wyoming Territory went unnoticed by the thousands of emigrants who crossed its barren expanses bound for points west on the Oregon-California Trail.

With the close of the Civil War and the completion of the Transcontinental Railroad in 1869, the sparsely populated Rocky Mountain West began to attract attention. Wyoming Territory was well suited to pastoral forms of agriculture, specifically cattle and sheep raising, since low land prices and free grass and water cut costs almost in half (Wentworth 1948:308–309).

Cattle empires dominated grazing for at least ten years prior to the advent of sheep in Wyoming (Vass and Pearson 1927:10), usurping prime areas of grass and water. The one exception was the vacant Red Desert adjacent to the Medicine Bow National Forest on the west; sheepmen quickly filled this void and remained dominant here throughout Wyoming's history (Wentworth 1948:538).

The sheep industry got underway in the late 1870s and early 1880s in this portion of Wyoming with such pioneers as Robert Taylor, Ike C. Miller, Frank Hadsell, the Savage Brothers, Fred Kindt, and William W. Daley. Walter and Richard Savage drove 5,000 to 6,000 sheep into the Rawlins region in 1882 or 1883, and quickly enlarged their operation, taking in more partners as the business increased (Wentworth 1948:316–317). One headquarters was located on North Cedar Creek just outside the present forest boundary. The Savage outfit was one of the first permittees on the Medicine Bow National Forest.

Fred Kindt arrived in 1885 and established his base of operations in Rawlins. He had at least 25,000 head of sheep in 1886 which he grazed "east of Pass Creek, above its junction with the North Platte." His summer grazing range was in the nearby Medicine Bows before the formation of the forest (Wentworth 1948:317). Kindt also grazed a large number of sheep in the Sierra Madres, and his name appears on the original list of permittees for the Hayden in 1907.

One of the larger sheep enterprises was conducted by the Cosgriff Brothers, who grazed as many as 125,000 sheep at peak periods. The Cosgriffs started near Fort Steele in 1882, relocated in Rawlins in 1885, and soon began purchasing the Union Pacific "checkerboard" lands between Hanna and Rawlins, thereby controlling access to intervening sections and the railroad. Their flocks ranged as far west as Rock Springs and Opal. This far flung network included supply houses for employees that gradually developed into a mercantile system of twelve to fifteen stores extending to Salt Lake City (Wentworth 1948:318).

Grazing on the Forest

Prior to the formation of the Medicine Bow National Forest, sheep and cattle had been grazed indiscriminately, with larger operations like the Cosgriff Brothers usurping the most range. The Sierra Madres had been so badly overgrazed that in 1916, Supervisor Blackhall stated:

> The grazing industry of this section is nearly extinct, brought on by overstocking, in fact with the exception of that portion which is protected by the long period that the snow lies on the ground, the short summer season and the early advent of winter, it may be said that the country is destitute of all forage necessary to support animal life . . . (Bruce 1959:51).

Gradually the Forest Service instituted grazing procedures designed to control the number of livestock using the forest each season and charging minimal grazing fees.

Grazing practices in the Medicine Bow area involved mov-

A Basin Land and Livestock Company outfit and range boss Charles Tomasek (mounted) hauling in supplies at Brooklyn Lake (1914). This outfit ran 6000 sheep on the Medicine Bow Forest.

The Ralston cabin, a high country sheep headquarters at the Brooklyn Lake Recreational Area.

ing livestock from lower elevation winter pastures to the nearby mountains for summer range. This procedure is known as transhumance, which first evolved among the Basque sheep herders in the Pyrenees Mountains (Cookson 1977:95–120). As the quantity of livestock was gradually reduced, formal grazing districts and allotments were established so that a certain number of sheep or cattle for each outfit grazed in a specified portion of the forest. Stock driveways were established throughout the forest, with counting corrals located at the boundaries.

The major driveways in the Sierra Madres were the Savery-Fireline Trail, the Deep Creek-Fireline Trail, the Elkhorn Driveway, the Encampment-Slater Driveway, and a small segment of the Hogpark Trail to Colorado. Counting corrals were established at the Trail Ranger Station and the Corral Ranger Station.

Medicine Bow Collection — American Heritage Center
Sheep operator E. Stratton and family, 1926 on the Encampment-Slater stock driveway, Hayden District. Note the use of the traditional sheep wagon.

A definite trailing schedule had been developed by 1914 to avoid delays in entering the forest (Ratliff 1935:7,822).

On the west side of the Medicine Bows, sheep were counted at the Savage Corrals near Wiant's Ranch on the Saratoga-Gold Hill Road and at the Cedar Creek corrals. The northern counting station was in Stanley Park on the Medicine Bow River on the road to Milo. The east entrance was on the North Fork of the Main Mill Creek, about six miles north of Centennial (Medicine Bow Collection).

The general grazing period for sheep was set from June 15 to September 30. The period of lambing ewes was May 5 to September 30. The charge was five cents a head and two additional cents for pregnant ewes. Cattle and horses grazed from April 15 to September 30, at twenty-five cents for the former and thirty-five cents for the latter (Wheeler 1913:6).

Medicine Bow Collection — American Heritage Center

National Forest grazing permits allow these day-old lambs and their mothers to enjoy the summer range in the Medicine Bows.

The Forest Service initiated management techniques which benefitted both the range and the livestock. The practice of "bedding out" was instituted for sheep. As Supervisor Lovejoy stated in 1909: "The sheep are stopped where they happen to be at night, the herder brings up his bed and the same performance continues practically all summer. In this way the sheep travel only about half as far for their day's feed as though they returned each night to the same bedding ground. Less travel of course means more feed." The Forest Service also instituted the practice of placing salt for cattle at strategic locations across allotments, so that the animals would be more evenly distributed.

Since the Laramie Peak District was not created until 1935, the better lands within the general boundary had already been

Medicine Bow Collection — American Heritage Center
Ranger Defler counts in a flock of sheep as it enters the forest at the Cedar Creek Corrals for the summer grazing season (1945).

Branding calves on the Medicine Bow National Forest, Spring, 1922.

filed upon. Forest Service lands therefore tend to be composed of "high rocky ridges"(Multiple Use Management Plan, Laramie Peak District 1968:1). The growing of cash crops has not been successful in this region due to short growing seasons and periodic drought conditions. Therefore, stock grazing is the chief concern of the population. Ranch headquarters are generally located along stream bottoms where the land can be irrigated for hay. Cattle, horses, and sheep are grazed in the high country during the summer season under permit, as in the other districts of the Medicine Bow National Forest.

The Taylor Grazing Act of July 28, 1934 effectively put an end to the public domain. Unappropriated public lands reverted back to the federal government. All public lands required grazing permits and were to be strictly regulated. According to T. A. Larson:

> This act, with a complimentary executive order, provided that the federal government would terminate home-steading except on reclamation projects, retain permanently its remaining public

lands, and regulate grazing thereon in the public interest (Larson 1965:136).

The Basque sheepherder was probably hardest hit by the act. In the early years of sheepherding, a practice known as "tramp herding" had developed, by which a herder could earn his wages in sheep, which remained with the employer's herd until the herder had enough sheep to start his own business. He would then send for a replacement by calling on a friend

Medicine Bow Collection — *American Heritage Center*
Sheepherders in Wyoming were often French or Spanish Basque immigrants. Those who earned their wages in sheep often became owners of large sheep operations themselves. Shown above is sheepherder Louie on the Jack Norton Ranch, 1964.

or relative in the Old Country. This system stimulated a steady flow of French and Spanish Basques to the U.S. However, it was dependent on free and open range, since the new Basque owner could not afford to buy or lease land (Cookson 1977:98–100). The Taylor Act removed the opportunity for the Basque herder to advance in this manner. As a result of the act and the immigration quota system, the sheep industry experienced a severe manpower shortage after 1934.

XI

GETTING FROM HERE TO THERE

MOST OF THE ROAD systems used today in the Medicine Bow National Forest are improvements upon and variations of old Indian and emigrant trails, such as the Overland, Cherokee, and Lodgepole Trails. The era of the tie hacks and miners saw the development of a crude road system in the late 1800s, but it was not until the recreation potential of the National Forests was recognized in the late teens and early twenties that intense road development occurred in the forest. Fire prevention was another motivating force in the construction of interior forest roads.

Trail

The Cherokee and Lodgepole Trails were two of the oldest transportation routes to pass in or near the forest. There were several variations of the Cherokee Trail; one major route skirted the Medicine Bows to the south, the other to the north (partially coinciding with the Overland Trail). Parts of the southern route appeared on General Land Office survey maps as early as 1870.

The northern variation of the Cherokee Trail passed near Tie Siding and headed toward Sheep Mountain, where it split. One branch headed north to McFadden, then southwest to Arlington, crossing the drainages flowing north out of the Medicine Bows. It crossed the North Platte at the mouth of Lake Creek, then proceeded up Jack Creek to Twin Groves, joining the southern route. The other variation appears to have entered the forest near Centennial, skirted the range to the

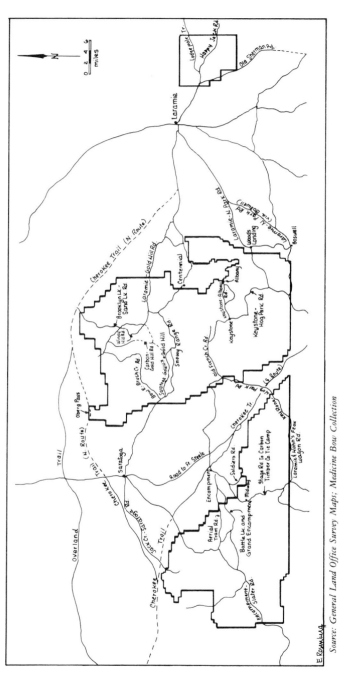

E. Roynnicry

Source: General Land Office Survey Maps; Medicine Bow Collection

Early transportation routes of the Medicine Bow National Forest.

north, and descended to the North Platte Valley via Pass Creek (Medicine Bow Collection).

The Lodgepole Trail entered the forest at the east boundary of the Pole Mountain Division. It generally followed the route of the present Forest Road #712 (Telephone Road) west and slightly south through the Pole Mountain area to its junction with the Happy Jack Road near the old ski area. It continued up the ridge north of the head of South Pole Creek, passing the site of Tie City. It then crossed Telephone Creek Draw just south of the junction of the Happy Jack Road and the main highway. It continued up a shallow draw, crossed a ridge south of Telephone Canyon (wagon ruts were reportedly still visible in Casper limestone on the west slope of this ridge in the 1950s), and finally joined the Overland Trail west of Laramie (Medicine Bow Collection).

Road

Pole Mountain

Branching off the Lodgepole Trail was the Old Sherman Road. It left the Salt Lake Stage Road (Lodgepole Trail or Cheyenne Pass Road) about one quarter mile east of the crest of the Laramie Mountains. It headed south-southeast along the southwest corner of the forest to the site of Sherman, a tie camp used to supply ties for the Union Pacific Railroad, and continued south to Virginia Dale.

A slightly later route through the Pole Mountain District connecting Laramie and Cheyenne was the Happy Jack Road. Named for Jack Hollingsworth, the route diverges from the Lodgepole Trail near Tie City in the northwest part of the district and swings southwest through the forest, passing through the northwest corner of the old Fort Francis E. Warren Target and Maneuver Reservation. Hollingsworth had a ranch near the foothills of the Laramie Range in the 1880s, and hauled wood from the mountains to sell in Cheyenne. He reportedly always sang as he worked (Writer's Project 1941:251).

Medicine Bow Collection — American Heritage Center

SNOWY RANGE ROAD

The deep drifts were hand shovelled in the late spring to gain the distinction of
being the "first over."

Medicine Bows

The Snowy Range Road (State Hwy. 130) from Laramie to the North Platte River was, and still is, the major east-west route through the main Medicine Bow Forest. The GLO survey plat of 1877 and 1879, shows a "Range Road" leaving from a point near Centennial, crossing Libby Creek and continuing along the north side of the creek. The GLO survey plat of 1898 shows a continuation of this road labeled "Centennial to La-Plata" which generally followed the route of the present highway and ended east of the pass. The earliest uses of this road were for timber and mining. The 1877 GLO plat shows a "Webber's Sawmill" in the approximate location of the present Centennial Ranger Station, indicating very early use of the area for timber production. Early tie camps were located along Libby Creek, Nash's Fork, and the North Fork of the Little Laramie. The route was used in connection with mining during the Gold Hill mining booms. There was also some mining activity around Libby Flats, formerly called LaPlata.

In 1909, Forest Supervisor P. S. Lovejoy requested $1,500 from the regional forester to cooperate on road improvements with the Albany County Commissioners and the Centennial Commercial Club. A combined total of $2,500 was raised, and the Laramie, Hahns Peak, and Pacific Railroad agreed to survey the Centennial-Snowy Range Wagon Road. In 1910, the first recorded auto trip took place between Centennial and Brooklyn Lake. Lovejoy drove a 1910 Franklin to Brooklyn Lake on Labor Day. The nine-mile trip took one hour (Medicine Bow Collection).

The forest began to develop its recreational potential in 1914. A reconnaissance was made in early 1915 for a route from Centennial to the Saratoga Road via Lake Marie and Brush Creek, and a rough but drivable road was constructed to Brooklyn Lake and Libby Flats.

A 1918 editorial predicted that the Snowy Range area would become one of the greatest pleasure resorts of the Rocky Mountains:

It has been inaccessible in the past, but the Forest Service is developing it in many ways. At present, the greatest need is a good road leading from Centennial with the base at Medicine Bow Peak and then on down to the Platte on the other side . . . The Forest Officers are willing anxious to give the patrons of the government good service, but have been prevented because of lack of funds. Roads cost money (*Laramie Republican Bomerang* 8/7/18).

The Forest Service reflected these sentiments, claiming that the current "wagon road" was not suitable for auto travel, and that the people of Albany County demanded a good road. Construction took place during the early 1920s, and dedication of the Snowy Range Road was held in July of 1926 (*Rawlins Reporter* 7/6/26).

In 1930, the route from Laramie to Saratoga was designed as a forest highway and during the 1930s, the entire route was black-topped. During the mid-to-late 1960s, both ends of Route 130 were improved with the western terminus changing from Saratoga to Days, and the eastern end following Nash Fork rather than the original route up Libby Creek (now known as the Barber Lake Road).

Agnes Wright Spring Collection
SNOWY RANGE ROAD
The "S" curves above the University of Wyoming Summer Science Camp.

Another important early road system in the area included the Laramie to North Park routes, via Boswell and Woods Landing. Pieces of these roads appear on the original GLO survey plats and on William Owen's 1886 map of Albany County. The first major route headed southwest out of Laramie, crossed the Big Laramie River at Riverside Ranch, continued southwest, and again crossed the Big Laramie at Boswell Ranch. It then proceeded up Boswell Creek, turned south across the state line near Mountain Home, and followed the present Route 230 through the neck of the park into Walden (Medicine Bow Collection). According to a letter written by a forest ranger in 1923, the Boswell-Mountain Home Road was used extensively by Mormons crossing the range to reach Salt Lake.

The Woods Landing-Mountain Home Road (present Route

Medicine Bow Collection — American Heritage Center
The Medicine Bow National Forest began to develop its recreational potential in the mid 'teens. Here, early campers enjoy the forest with an elaborate camp, complete with waving American flag.

230) cut off 14.2 miles from the original Laramie-North Park Road. The portion of this route between Woods Landing and Chimney Park was built by Sam Woods, an early sawmiller. The route was used as a stage road, with daily service between Laramie and North Park until around 1910 when the railroad reached Walden. Stage stations were established every twelve miles, and Woods Landing was one of the major stops. There was also a route between Woods Landing and the Boswell

Medicine Bow Collection — American Heritage Center
This eight-pound trout was caught at Lake Marie in July, 1920.

Ranch, via Jelm, that followed the Big Laramie and was used as a daily stage route. Around 1908-1912, when autos were first used, the original Boswell Route was more popular, and the Woods Landing Route was used only by wood haulers.

Four of the earliest roads on the Medicine Bow were instigated by the Gold Hill mining boom of the late 1880s. In 1889, four towns began construction in late October, at the height of the rush, on roads leading to the district. The Laramie-Gold Hill road followed the Middle Fork of Mill Creek, and used old tie roads extending several miles up Mill Creek. At 10,000 feet, they cut a new road through three miles of lodgepole timber. The road was then constructed over a saddle between the North Fork of the Little Laramie and the head of Rock Creek, then turned south toward Brooklyn Lake and around the southern end of the high peaks of the Snowies to Gold Hill. A group from Arlington raced toward Gold Hill via a ridge north of Rock Creek from Arlington to Sand Lake, passing Windy Hill on the west and thence to Gold Hill. This route was known as the Windy Hill Road. Coal miners from Carbon headed toward Gold Hill by way of the Medicine Bow River, entering the forest near the Bow River Station. The group from Saratoga won the race, arriving at Gold Hill before their competitors via the Saratoga-Gold Hill Road. The route involved a shorter distance and easier terrain, but more snow. Approximately twelve miles of the road were cut through timber at elevations ranging from 8,100-10,000 feet (Medicine Bow Collection).

The "Old French Creek Road" appears on GLO survey plats from 1877-78, surveyed by William O. Downey. During the late 1890s when a smelter was planned at Encampment, a wagon road was built from the Rambler mine in the Keystone Mining District to Encampment to haul ore from the mine to the smelter (Medicine Bow Collection).

Roads were built in several directions from Keystone, the center of the mining activity. One was constructed in the 1870s from Keystone to Hog Park by Mortimer N. Grant, a pioneer mining engineer and surveyor. Until the 1890s, this was one of the two roads from the Little Snake River to Laramie, and was shorter than the North Park Road.

Numerous timber roads were in use throughout the main Medicine Bow by the late 1800s. Some of these were later developed into recreational roads still in use, but many have simply disappeared. Some of these timber roads were located in the northeast portion of the forest in the vicinity of Mill Creek, Sevenmile Creek, and Fourmile Creek. A great deal of road construction and maintenance occurred during the 1930s and early 1940s through the Civilian Conservation Corps program.

Sierra Madres

As in most mountainous areas, the earliest roads in the Sierra Madres Region served the mining and timber industries. According to E. C. Peryam in a newspaper article in 1934,

Medicine Bow Collection — American Heritage Center
An early version of the four-wheel drive tries out the bridge over Carlson Creek.

there was an old wagon road connecting a fort near Encampment with a lumber camp seven miles up the Encampment River. The fort was reportedly built in the 1860s to protect loggers supplying the Union Pacific Railroad and Fort Steele from hostile Indians. The site was described as being about three-fourths of a mile above the present town of Riverside. About three-fourths of a mile west of the fort was the Soldiers Road, a wagon trail used by the government in the 1860s to supply the logging camp established to provide lumber for building Fort Steele, although other accounts indicate that Elk Mountain was the source of wood for construction of Fort Steele (Peryam, 1934).

The earliest serious mining activity in the area occurred in 1881 at the Doane-Rambler Mine. Since Encampment did not exist until 1898, ore was probably hauled north to Fort Steele. A strike in Purgatory Gulch in 1897 attracted miners to the area. The following year the Ferris-Haggarty Copper Mine at Rudefeha was established, and Encampment was built. Other

Medicine Bow Collection — American Heritage Center   *Photo by H. C. Hilton*
Ranger Williams clears felled timber from the Centennial-Arlington Trail in 1925.

mining communities in the area were Copperton, Rambler, and Battle (Junge 1792).

In 1902, a smelter was built in Encampment, as well as a sixteen-mile long aerial tramway to connect the smelter with the mine at Rudefeha. A road closely paralleling the tramway appears on a United States Geological Survey map (surveyed in 1901 and included in a 1904 study) and was probably used in the construction of the tramway. By 1905, the isolated mining camps were served by a stage route. The Scribner Stage Company ran stages (six-horse Concord coaches) from Walcott Junction to Saratoga and Encampment, leaving Walcott daily at 7:00 A.M. From Encampment, daily stages served Battle, 12 miles away; Rambler, 14 miles; Dillon, 19 miles; and Copperton, 20 miles. One could obtain saddle horses or livery teams to connect with the Holmes-Laramie stage line at the New Rambler mine 32 miles east of Encampment. Connections by team could also be made from Rawlins for Dillon and Rudefeha, 52 miles distant. Dillon and Rudefeha also benefited from a daily (except Sunday) mail and stage line from Saratoga (Beeler 1905:5).

Mining camps in the vicinity of Spring Creek and Jack Creek at the north end of the range were also accessible from Saratoga. Freight was generally brought in on the Walcott-Saratoga-Encampment Road and then distributed to the camps in the region. There was no railroads, so wagon roads were essential to the development of the region. As of 1905, over five hundred miles of wagon roads had been built in the Encampment District to connect the various camps to nearby towns and to each other (Beeler 1905:5).

During the summer of 1902, the Carbon Timber Company established a major tie camp on the South Fork of the Encampment River near the Colorado state line (possibly just over the border) in Encampment Meadows. Forty-five men were put to work constructing a wagon road from the sawmill on Green Mountain to the new tie camp via Hog Park. It would serve not only the tie camp of some three hundred men, but also the miners of the Hog Park area who had needed such a road for many months *(The Grand Encampment Herald* 7/25/1902, 8/1/1902).

By the end of August 1902, a daily mail and stage route was established between the new tie camp and Grand Encampment, making a total of four regular stage routes in and out of that town. Construction was also underway on a half-way station on Green Mountain, referred to as Olsen or Midway. A large force of men was enlisted to work on the town. This tie camp road connected with the Laramie and Hahn's Peak wagon road, establishing a link between Grand Encampment and Routt County, Colorado *(The Grand Encampment Herald* 8/29/02).

Frank White was the stage driver on the Grand Encampment-tie camp road in 1904. The stage ran year round, three times a week, to and from the tie camp. White would get to the half-way house in the afternoon, then start for the tie camp early the following morning, arriving about noon *(The Grand-Encampment Herald* 12/30/04).

Laramie Range

Early transportation routes in the Laramie Peak area served to connect the Union Pacific Railroad with military installations. The Fort Fetterman and Rock Creek stage road connected Rock Creek Station on the Union Pacific with Fort Fetterman (about ten miles northwest of present day Douglas), then continues north and northwest to Fort McKinney, Wyoming, and Fort Custer, Montana.

A thirty-six-mile stretch of good road ran from the railroad to the summit of the pass in the Laramie Hills. The next thirty-eight miles to LaPrele Creek, at the northern base of the Laramie Hills, were "very steep and bad." The road then followed the LaPrele Valley to Fort Fetterman. In 1877, this road was opened as a replacement for the road from Medicine Bow Station which ran northward to its junction with the Rock Creek road, fourteen miles south of Fort Fetterman. The Rock

Creek road was gentler and on firmer soil, a few miles shorter, and had fewer streams to cross between the railroad and the summit (U.S. Congress, House 1879: 1708–9).

The Fort Fetterman and Rock Creek stage road appears on the General Land Office maps, surveyed in the early 1880s. Two stage stations appear in the vicinity of the National Forest, the Fortymile Ranch, and the Point of Rocks Station.

The road between Medicine Bow and Fort Fetterman was used until 1877, when it was replaced by the Fort Fetterman and Rock Creek stage road. This route was 85.4 miles long, and included a very hilly stretch of 45 miles (crossing the Laramie Hills south of Fort Fetterman). Fourteen miles of the route lay in canyons and were heavily snowed under from November to May. The last 40 miles, covering the Laramie Plains, involved four river crossings and areas of poor grass and no wood (U.S. Congress, House 1879: 1724).

This route appears on GLO maps surveyed in the early 1880s as the "Medicine Bow-Fort Fetterman Wagon Road." It crosses the Medicine Bow Forest from southwest to northeast, generally following Box Elder Creek.

Another early major route in the Laramie Peak area was the road from Fort Laramie to Rock Creek Station. Sections of the route east and west of the Laramie Hills were reportedly well traveled and good, and were connected by "an extremely favorable but untraveled pass through the hills" (U.S. Congress, House 1879: 1729). This route established an easy line of communication between Fort Laramie and the Laramie Plains.

The road entered the forest in the vicinity of Cottonwood Creek near the east boundary, then swung south, passing a few miles to the east of Laramie Peak. It crossed the North Laramie River and continued south and west, joining the Fort Fetterman and Rock Creek road about two miles from the Rock Creek Station. Most of this route appears on GLO maps surveyed in the early 1880s, and is roughly followed today by US Forest Route 633 as far north as Black Mountain, where it heads east at Cottonwood Creek.

Rail

Medicine Bow National Forest's only railroad was the Laramie, Hahns Peak and Pacific Railway, known over the years by six different official names. Due to its almost constant problems, the line was also known as the "Late, Hard Pressed and Panicky" and the "Lord Help Push and Pull." In 1880, the Laramie, North Park and Pacific Railroad, and the Pacific Railroad and Telegraph Company were incorporated by a group of Albany County men. They proposed to construct a railroad from Laramie southwest to Soda Lakes, thence to the Medicine Bows to follow the Big Laramie to a tributary affording access across the range. It would then connect with the Grand River Valley Railroad in Carbon County. In actuality, it reached only as far as Soda Lakes west of Laramie, where it served the mining community there for several years (Homsher 1949:55–56).

The standard gauge railroad, originally known as the Laramie Plains Line, got off to a bad start financially, but managed to survive most of its contemporaries. The original promoter and builder was Isaac Van Horn of Boston, who organized the Laramie, Hahns Peak and Pacific Railway Company early in 1901, when a frenzy of empire building hit Laramie and Albany Counties. The goal was to reach the mining area of Gold Hill in the Snowy Range. It would then descend the range, cross the upper Platte Valley, and proceed to Grand Encampment, Battle Lake, and Steamboat Springs (Hollenback 1960).

Before any rails were laid, promoter Van Horn began to develop Centennial, establishing a fish hatchery, golf course, and clubhouse. The stockbrokers realized the railroad was engaged in every activity but railroading, and it was not until 1907 that the train reached Centennial. By then, the Gold Hill and Centennial area mines had fizzled, and the LHP&P turned south toward North Park. The railroad purchased seven square miles of a rich coal deposit near Walden called Coalmont (*Rock River Review:* "Laramie Had A Railroad of its Own" by Kenneth Jessen, n.d.). The railroad would transport timber from the Medicine Bows and coal from North Park. The nearest railroads at the time of construction were the Union Pacific at Laramie and the Moffat Road to the south at Granby in Middle Park, so the line would provide a needed route into North Park. The first train reached Centennial on June 17, 1907. One train a day ran between Laramie and Centennial. Between 1907 and 1914, the line was also known as the Larimer and Routt County Railway Company (Hollenback 1906).

After 1907, about ten miles of track were laid per year. Sixteen horses and a grading machine were needed to build the horseshoe curve above Albany, at a cost of $21,000 (Hollenback 1960). Track laying operations increased as winter approached, and the first train from Laramie reached Walden on October 25, 1911. Coalmont, the western terminus, was reached in December, completing the one hundred eleven-mile line. Winter operating costs were so high that the mortgage could not be paid, and in 1914, the line was forced to sell. The Colorado, Wyoming and Eastern Railroad took control, but severe winters continued to plague the line. During the winter of 1917, it took twenty-one days to complete a single Laramie-Coalmont round trip.

The railroad changed names twice in 1924. In April, new owners called the line the Northern Colorado and Eastern Railroad Company. At the urging of city residents, Laramie was again added to the name, and in June it became the Laramie, North Park, and Western Railroad Company.

During the 1930s, the Interstate Commerce Commission requested that the Union Pacific take over the struggling line. Although they were reluctant to do so, a merger was consummated in 1935. In 1941, the Union Pacific petitioned to abandon the line (many short lines were being abandoned around this time, often for the iron in the rails). The ICC denied the petition. During and after World War II, the line continued to freight timber, coal, livestock, and minerals.

In 1951, the line became the Coalmont Branch of the Union Pacific. As a result, the name of Laramie, North Park and Western was dissolved, the Laramie depot was closed, and operations were handled from the Laramie depot of the Union Pacific. Tri-weekly service between Laramie and Coalmont was to continue. The Coalmont branch of the Union Pacific is still an active railroad (Hollenback 1960).

XII.

FIGHTING THE DEPRESSION: CIVILIAN CONSERVATION CORPS

THE CIVILIAN CONSERVATION CORPS played an important role in the nation's forests in the 1930s and early 1940s. The Medicine Bow National Forest benefited greatly from the program.

In March 1933, Congress responded to President Roosevelt's urgings by creating the Civilian Conservation Corps under the Unemployment Relief Act. The CCC proved to be one of the most popular New Deal agencies, providing employment for almost 3 million young men during the program's existence. Roosevelt had hoped to place the CCC program on a permanent basis; however, the manpower demands of World War II made this unrealistic by 1942. The program was designed to meet the major objectives of economic relief (all but five dollars of the enrollee's thirty dollar monthly check was sent to his dependents on relief, thereby recirculating money back into the cities), restoring confidence and "building men," and also resulted in a large amount of beneficial and lasting work (Medicine Bow Collection).

The camps operated at varying strengths from 1933 through 1942, under the direct supervision of the U.S. Army. The men often came from large cities and poor families, and the sudden transfer to a wilderness environment and harsh climate must have been difficult. Instances of violence may not have been commonplace, but at least two suicides and a fatal knife attack were reported to have occurred within the Medicine Bow CCC camps.

Selection of enrollees involved several requirements. The age limit was initially 18–25, but was apparently modified over the years. As of 1935, age limits were reportedly 18–35, by 1937, 17–28, and then 17–23, although World War I veterans were exempt from the upper age limit (*Laramie Republican-Boomerang* (6/28/37). The men were required to be physically fit, unmarried, and unemployed United States citizens who had dependents to whom they were willing to allot most of their pay of $30 per month.

Selection began from names on relief lists. The program sought men of character: clean cut, purposeful, and ambitious. Enrollment was totally voluntary, and there was no discrimination as to race, creed, color, or politics. The men were supervised by the U.S. Army, but were under no military discipline or drills, nor wore Army uniforms (Medicine Bow Collection).

An enrollee entered the CCC for a term of six months, and could then reenter until he had served two years. Each camp consisted of about two hundred men under the supervision of a commanding officer. Headquarters for Wyoming camps were operated out of Fort Francis E. Warren in Cheyenne.

Facilities varied somewhat from camp to camp, but most of the camps had barracks, a kitchen, a mess hall, latrines, showers or baths (often with hot and cold running water), a recreation room, and officers' quarters. Other facilities sometimes included a reading room, a blacksmith shop, tennis courts, and areas for baseball and football. Most camps generated their own electricity, and newsreels and motion pictures were often available. One of the camps even boasted a small orchestra (*Laramie Daily Bulletin* 10/31/81).

In addition to the CCC camps, Medicine Bow also had two transient relief camps, which were established by the Emergency Relief Act (ERA). These men, at Pole Mountain and Mountain Home, worked under the supervision of the U.S. Forest Service, but were housed and paid by the Relief Administration. Also under the ERA, men on Laramie relief rolls were employed and paid by the Forest Service (Armstrong 1935:31–32).

Wyoming CCC camps were part of the Eighth Corps Area, which also included Texas, Arizona, New Mexico, Colorado, and Oklahoma. The first camp in Wyoming was established at Pole Mountain on May 15, 1933. Six others followed: Chimney Park (F-17), Centennial, Arlington, Encampment (F-21), Ryan Park (F-22), and French Creek (Medicine Bow Collection).

At the end of the 1933 season, there were 835 men enrolled in seven Wyoming CCC camps. Most of the camps were seasonal, with men working in warmer climates during the winter months and returning the following May. Other camps that came and went in the region of the Medicine Bow National Forest throughout the years of the program included Brush Creek camp (F-39), Mullen Creek camp (F-36), Esterbrook camp (F-37), and Saratoga Hot Springs (State Park) camp (F-38). Men were continually being transferred back and forth among the camps, and often "side camps" were established for specific projects.

Types of work varied from camp to camp, but the tasks generally included the following: maintenance and construction

Medicine Bow Collection — American Heritage Center
A telephone construction crew takes a break at the Rambler Ranger Station.

of trails, roads, bridges, fences, telephone lines, ranger stations, camp grounds and picnic grounds, fire lookout stations, and winter sports areas, as well as rodent and insect control, thinning of timber, erosion control, and fire fighting (*Laramie Daily Bulletin* 10/21/38). Roadside cleanup was done by all camps to improve attractiveness and reduce fire hazard (Medicine Bow Collection).

A few of the CCC's many valuable projects included the following: Research plots were established at the Chimney Park camp, where trees would be measured every five years to compare growth with unthinned stands. Working in cooperation with the Fish and Game Department, CCC camps built retaining or rearing ponds for fish cultures at Towner Lake, at the millpond below Towner Lake, on Muddy Creek, on Upper Brush Creek, and at Pole Mountain. Many existing campgrounds were improved, enlarged, and fireproofed. Vedauwoo Glen camp ground on Pole Mountain was enlarged to twenty

Medicine Bow Collection — American Heritage Center
Medicine Bow National Forest hosted several CCC camps during the Depression, and many of their improvements are still visible. Here, men from the Ryan Park CCC camp construct a bridge across Barrett Creek in 1933.

times its original size. Other improvements included sanitation and conveniences: latrines, tables, grates, water, and shelter. In November 1938, work was begun by the Saratoga CCC on the new winter sports course on Barrett Ridge in Ryan Park, near Medicine Bow Lodge (*Wyoming State Tribune* 11/17/38). CCC enrollees, with local help, planted some 280,000 ponderosa and lodgepole pines on four hundred acres of denuded land on Pole Mountain. Seedlings were supplied by the Pole Mountain Nursery (*Laramie Republican-Boomerang* 4/18/38).

Around 1935, the University of Wyoming instituted a program of correspondence courses for some four hundred CCC workers in Wyoming. Dr. J. R. MacNeel, correspondence study director, prepared courses in English, math, social sciences, biology, typing, and shorthand which were already in the university files. Prepared especially for the CCC were courses in auto mechanics, elementary forestry, journalism, and bookkeeping. Studying was to be done during the "leisure hours" and during bad weather, under the supervision of camp educational

Medicine Bow Collection — American Heritage Center   *Photo by H. C. Hilton*

Early road work in the forest was done with the help of mules and fresno.

advisors and the technical staff. Funds for this program were provided by the Works Progress Administration (Medicine Bow Collection).

Work continued into the 1940s. In November 1940, Saratoga CCC camp (F-38) was still working on the Barrett Ridge winter sports area, the South Brush Creek picnic ground, and range fence construction. The Mullen Creek CCC was working on range fences and thinning lodgepole. The Pole Mountain CCC side camp was erecting fences on the north side of the Lincoln Highway to keep people out of the military maneuver area, which was strictly closed to the public (*Laramie Daily Bulletin* 11/29/40).

The year 1941 proved to be the last full active season for the CCC. During that year, work commenced on the Libby Creek Ski Area by a side camp at Centennial from Chimney Park (*Laramie Republican-Boomering* 12/20/41). At Esterbrook Camp (F-37), 127 men worked on the Eagle Peak truck trail. Both the Brush Creek and Mullen Creek CCC camps were scheduled to close during 1941. Brush Creek personnel had spent two summers at Ryan Park, five winters at Saratoga Hot Springs State Park, and four winters at Esterbrook. Their accomplishments had included 127 miles of phone lines, the Esterbrook fire lookout, and the Libby Creek Ski Area (Medicine Bow Collection). The Mullen Creek Camp had operated for three years, and had worked on the lengthy boundary fence for Sheep Mountain under Capt. Vernon, the commanding officer. Their facilities had included a blacksmith shop, library, tennis court, and garage (Medicine Bow Collection). The Chimney Park camp, which had operated continuously since 1933, was the last camp to close. It was disbanded on July 20, 1942 (*Laramie Daily Bulletin* 7/16/42). The site of the Ryan Park CCC camp was later used during World War II as a prisoner of war compound (*Wyoming State Tribune* 7/14/60).

The Mullen Creek camp, closed during the early years of World War II, was renovated in 1943 for use as an Army-Air Force rest camp. It was enjoyed by several hundred men before shutting down in August 1945 (Wiegand 1976:72). It was eventually acquired by the University of Wyoming, which used it as a recreational camp and gradually replaced the original log buildings (Wiegand 1976:75). The Centennial Ranger Station is concurrently located in the general area of the Mullen Creek CCC camp.

XIII.

TAKING TO THE HILLS

Resorts and Lodges

THE RECREATIONAL POTENTIAL of Medicine Bow National Forest was not recognized until around 1914. The advent of the automobile made the previously remote wilderness more accessible to the public, and the Forest Service began to respond to the needs of the people to experience the benefits of an unspoiled environment.

Snowy Range Lodge

One of the most spectacular and well known of the resort lodges was the Snowy Range Lodge, also known as Libby Lodge. It is located about three miles from Centennial, and one mile on the Barber Lake Road from the junction of Libby Creek camp ground and Route 130. In 1924, the Snowy Range Resort Company announced plans to build a resort at Silver City, the site of an old mining camp. Architect W. A. Hitchcock planned a large main wing with 13 rooms on the second floor and 4 on the third floor. The main floor was to be used for a dining area, dance hall, offices, and a kitchen. A two story wing (to be set at a 45 degree angle to the main wing) would contain 24 bedrooms. Logs were already cut and hewn. The complex was to include the main hotel and 12 cabins. It was expected that ten thousand dollars would completely cover the cost of the construction. The grand opening was anticipated for June 1924 which would "mark the beginning of another Estes Park" (*Laramie Republican-Boomering* 1/7/24). The opening was presumably delayed until 1925, at which time the Laramie papers announced that construction was almost completed. The

LIBBY LODGE (Snowy Range Lodge), 1927
It was constructed in 1925 utilizing 7000 hand-peeled native trees and imported hardwood flooring. The Libby Lodge is an excellent example of early 20th Century resort lodge construction.

resort would accommodate up to 76 people, 44 in cabins, and 32 in the lodge (*Laramie Republican-Boomering* 6/20/25).

Libby Lodge has been described as an excellent example of turn of the century resort lodge construction. Seven thousand hand-peeled and chinked native trees were used. The floors were of imported hardwood. The three story rock fireplace was reportedly built by Anthony "Pop" Schlotzer, a local sculptor. In 1926, the Forest Service granted the lodge a ninety-nine-year lease under a special use permit (Chadey 1979:1,25).

The lodge remained in use through 1974. From 1974 to 1977, the building was vacant, deteriorating badly, and was seriously vandalized. David Egolf of Laramie purchased the structure in 1977, and in 1979 began restoration at his own expense. He is operating under a special use permit from the Forest Service, and plans to restore the building to its original appearance. The building is on the National Register of Historic Places (David Egolf, Personnal Communication 1981).

Two versions relate an Indian attack near the site of Libby Lodge. A tie camp, operated by from 1868–1869, was located on the site of the lodge. Mounted Indians from the prairies attacked the tie hacks, who fled to the woods. All reportedly survived, but all the camp buildings were burned, and the camp was never rebuilt. The office and commissary reportedly stood on the site of the lodge kitchen. Remains of the tie camp cabins were reported to have been observed in 1946 (Junge 1976).

The other version involved the temporary mining camp of Silver City, supposedly located where the lodge now stands. No date was mentioned for the incident, but it was reported that Indians had attacked miners about one-half mile from the camp. All were killed except for young Claude May, who had been out gathering wood (Wiegand 1976:32). Neither version has been verified.

Medicine Bow Lodge

Medicine Bow Lodge was one of the other early and well-known resorts located on the west side of the Snowy Range. It was built in 1917 on Barrett Creek in Ryan Park, just off Route 130, about two miles east of the west boundary of the main Medicine Bow Division. Medicine Bow Lodge was constructed by Sisson and Moore, and opened on July 15, 1917 as a private hunting lodge. By the early 1920s, it was operating as a summer guest ranch, kicking off each new season with a big dance.

A pamphlet issued by the Union Pacific Railroad in 1937 advertised the ranch as having accommodations for one hundred fifty guests in twenty-six cabins, single or double, also bath houses with hot and cold water. The menu included fresh butter, eggs, milk, vegetables, and meat.

Medicine Bow Lodge reportedly has not missed a season

since opening in 1917, making it the earliest as well as the longest continually operating resort in the forest. The original lodge and fireplace are still being used, along with new cabins and additions. It can accommodate about thirty-six people, and operates as a guest ranch in the summer and as a resort for cross-country skiers and snowmobilers in the winter (Medicine Bow Lodge Management, Personal Communication 1981).

Echo Lodge

Echo Lodge, also known as the Roper Place, is one of the oldest lodges in the forest. The Echo Lodge complex covers about twenty-two acres. It is located along Smith North Creek, a tributary of Douglas Creek. It is situated on National Forest

Medicine Bow Lodge, built in 1917, was one of the earliest resorts in the forest, and featured a main lodge and numerous small cabins. The original lodge and fireplace are still in use; the resort is the oldest continuously operating one in the forest.

land, and after many years of private ownership, it is now the property of the Forest Service.

Billy Roper, born in the 1850s, came west from Elmira, New York, because of a respiratory ailment. He worked on the Union Pacific Railroad, in the Colorado mines, and finally in the Keystone area mines (Beery n.d.:2). He built himself a sturdy cabin (15-by-25-feet) out of hand-hewn notched logs in 1884. The lodge itself was built by Roper aided by a team of horses, using 4-by-4's and 4-by-6's. He received help from the Muddy Creek Tie Camp for setting the rafters. He also built a cabin across the creek, and two more cabins and a barn. His original barn is now gone; another barn and two additional cabins were built in 1933, after Roper's death.

Roper made his lodge available to itinerant miners of the area, as well as to tie hacks working on tie drives and rented three of his cabins to summer fishermen. He cleared about twenty acres for raising hay for his horses and tame deer. His establishment was also reportedly used as the site for a sawmill until 1910 (Kerr and Rudkin 1979:1). Roper was employed by the Wyoming Timber Company every spring to watch for log jams on the tie drives, and earned $4.79 a day. He was known to be well educated and have a large library of classics. He never married and lived a fairly solitary life. When the Forest Service indicated the Roper place on their maps as a Ranger Station, he became so angry, he once ran Forest Supervisor H. C. Hilton off his land. The Forest Service reportedly did not approach him again (Kerr and Rudkin 1979:4).

In 1923, Tommy and Edith Thomson moved to the Keystone area and helped Roper run the lodge. In 1925, they began operating a summer camp for boys aged 8–12 with respiratory ailments (Berry n.d.:3). Roper died in 1932 and left the complex to the Thomsons, who were issued a special use permit by the Forest Service. They built the existing barn and two more cabins, as well as some additions to the main lodge after Roper's death. In 1947 the Thomsons sold their interest to Bernice and Raymond Doll of Cheyenne. The Dolls named the resort Echo Lodge and continued to run it on a special use permit until 1977.

Brooklyn Lodge

Brooklyn Lodge was the creation of Harry "Hoot" Jones, an ex–rodeo cowboy who worked on the road crew building the Snowy Range Road in 1923. While he was working on the road, he selected a spot for a mountain lodge. In 1924, he built Brooklyn Lodge and the accompanying cabins south of the highway across from Brooklyn Lake. He opened each summer season with a dance that lasted until breakfast the following morning.

According to an illustrated pamphlet distributed by the Union Pacific Railroad in 1937, accommodations at Brooklyn Lodge included twenty-five cabins, as well as the main lodge. Recollections of two Forest Rangers tend to refute the large number of cabins; they felt there were probably no more than a dozen, so perhaps the advertising was somewhat exaggerated (Stratten Van and Terry Hoffman, Personal Communications, 1981). The pamphlet further boasted of bath houses with hot and cold showers, a large central hall for dining and dancing, a large living room with cheerful fireplaces, a playhouse for children, a registered nurse in residence, and no snakes (Union Pacific Railroad Pamphlet 1937).

Brooklyn Lodge is located at 10,130-feet elevation, about eight miles west of Centennial on National Forest land. The main lodge is situated on the south side of Route 130, and houses the staff; the guest cabins are located on the north side of the highway. Having deteriorated badly by the early 1970s, the original cabins on the south side were torn down and replaced with new cabins on the north side.

Other Resorts

Two resorts of note in the Medicine Bows were the Thompson Lodge, located near Douglas Creek, and the Sand Lake Resort, located at Sand Lake on the Arlington Road, which was built around 1924. The latter included several cabins, twenty-nine acres of pasture, and the Snowy Range Fishing Lodge (*Rock River Review* 12/3/25). Charles Crismore ran the resort for many years, and accumulated a collection of numerous Indian artifacts from the Sand Lake area (Medicine Bow Collection). Sand Lake Lodge, as of 1981, is still operating as a summer resort (Terry Hoffman, Personal Communcation 1981).

The Summit Inn, originally called the Grenville Dodge Inn, was built in 1926 at the summit of the Lincoln Highway and was dedicated to Grenville Dodge, the builder of the railroad (*Wyoming Stockman Farmer* 9/26). It was operated under a Forest Service permit, and in 1928 was expected to be serving meals, and renting cabins and saddle horses. It appears on a 1929 Forest Service map as the "Summit Inn."

A 1940 photo shows an attractive, rambling, one-story log building. It provided food and drink for skiers at the Summit Ski Area, at least through the late 1940s (Union Pacific Railroad Pamphlet n.d). The Summit Inn has since burned down, and no traces remain (Terry Hoffman, Personal Communication 1981).

Environment as Education

The 12 to 15 miles between Centennnial and Medicine Bow Peak cross four life zones: the Arctic-Alpine, Hudsonian, Canadian, and Transition. The science departments at the University of Wyoming in Laramie realized the instructional potential of such an environment. Before 1925, Dr. J. W. Scott, head of the zoology department, promoted the use of Sheep Mountain as a base for a natural area and as a location for a summer science camp. However, the site chosen was south of Route 130 on the edge of the Snowy Range Natural Area between the Green Rock Picnic Ground and the Brooklyn Lake Road.

The "Coolest Summer School in America" was organized in 1922 to offer courses in geology, zoology, botany, forestry, and engineering. Officers of the Forest Service were requested to give weekend lectures on the Medicine Bow National Forest and forestry practices. The Director of the Summer Science Camp for many years was Dr. S. H. Knight, head of the University of Wyoming geology department (*Laramie Republican-Boomerang* 3/27/26).

In 1927, the forest granted the university a special use permit (revised in 1935) to cover the use of 26.5 acres for construction and maintenance of one main lodge building, two laboratory buildings, and thirty-five service and miscellaneous buildings. In 1935, an area of 771 acres of virgin timber near the camp was set aside as a natural area for conducting studies of soil structure and chemical composition, geology, botany, forest ecology, etc. The project attracted many prominent researchers and insured the protection and preservation of virgin spruce timber.

As of 1951, the summer camp was still under the supervision of Dr. S. H. Knight, and was reportedly used by students and faculty from all over the country. The institution remained active until the mid-1970s, when the considerable operating expenses and deterioration of buildings could no longer justify its existence. The high altitude and almost year round snow had long made the camp's functioning difficult. In 1981, the university sold the camp to the University of the Wilderness, a private concern, for a nominal sum. The latter will provide courses in environmental education and ecological studies. The camp was nominated for the National Register of Historic Places by the State of Wyoming in 1980 (Terry Hoffman, Personal Communication 1981).

Winter Sports

The late 1930s and early 1940s saw a surge in the development of winter sports areas. At least five areas were thriving during this period, three on the main Medicine Bow and two on Pole Mountain.

The plans for the Barrett Ridge (or Ryan Park) winter sports area were announced by the Forest Service in November 1938. It was to be developed near the Medicine Bow Lodge, and labor was to be furnished by the Saratoga CCC camp (*Wyoming State Tribune* 11/17/38). Barrett Ridge opened the winter of 1941–1942 with a chair lift 2,600-feet long with forty chairs (*Laramie Bulletin* 12/11/41). Cross country skiing trails were also available (Union Pacific Railroad Pamphlet, n.d.). Barrett Ridge reportedly ended operations in the 1960s (Medicine Bow Lodge management, personal communication 10/23/81).

The Libby Creek Area was located about 1.5 miles above Libby Lodge, off what is now the Barber Lake Road (originally the route of Highway 130), not far from the Inspiration Point Ski Area (*Laramie Republican-Boomerang* 2/26/40). The area was developed by the Brush Creek CCC camp enrollees (clipping 10/28/41; Medicine Bow Collection, Scrapbook). The slopes were located at a 9,200-foot elevation, and the main run was over three-fourths of a mile long with a 25–60 percent slope. A chair lift 3,000 feet long and two rope tows serviced the area. A practice slope was located close to a log shelter cabin built by the Forest Service. The Snowy Range Winter Sports Club operated the ski tows and offered instructions. Cross country ski runs were also available, one of which was eight miles long and led to a "sensational slalom run off the Snowy Range to Brooklyn Lake." There were also toboggan runs (Union Pacific Railroad Pamphlet, n.d.). Libby Creek was closed during the war, revived for a period of time after the war, then closed in 1953 (Wiegand 1976:75). Remains of the steep, narrow slopes of the Libby Creek Area can still be seen from the Barber Lake Road.

Inspiration Point was another ski area located near the Libby Creek Area, somewhere below Lake Marie (*Laramie Republican-Boomerang* 2/26/40). It apparently opened the winter of 1938–1939, when the Snowy Range Winter Sports Club tried out the new ski lift (*Laramie Republican-Boomering* 12/25/38). A shelter cabin was constructed that winter, measuring 20-by-24-feet. Newspaper clippings indicated that the ski area was still used in 1940, but no date of abandonment or exact location was available. From available information gathered, it seems likely that Inspiration Point was also referred to as the Snowy Range Winter Sports Area (*Laramie Republican-Boomering2/26/40*; WPA writers project. 1941:256).

One of the winter sports areas on Pole Mountain was the Happy Jack area, located eleven miles from Laramie on the Happy Jack Road at the head of Pole Creek. The approach to the area put the skiers at a point slightly higher than the top of the runs, saving a strenuous climb from the bottom.

It appears that the run lacked any kind of a tow at the time that the Mullen Creek CCC side camp worked on the area in 1938 (*Laramie Republican-Boomerang* 1/14/38). There is some evidence to suggest that the Pole Mountain CCC camp also worked on it (taped testimony of 1940 CCC enrollee R. J. Smith 1981). Use of slides and runs was regulated by a Forest Service caretaker. In addition to a 1,500-foot slalom run and a practice slope, there was a 1,400-foot ice-trough toboggan run (WPA Writers' Project 1941). The Happy Jack winter sports area may have also been referred to as the Pole Mountain Ski Area. It was closed in 1977 (Terry Hoffman, Personal Communications 1981).

The Summit Ski Area was also located on Pole Mountain, at the highest point on the Lincoln Highway. It was in use the winter of 1939–1940 (*Laramie Republican-Boomerang* 2/26/40). The elevation was 8,500 feet, and the Summit Tavern (Summit Inn), located at the top of the area, provided food and drink. One 825-foot tow rope, with a 200-foot rise as well as cross-country trails, was available to skiers (Union Pacific Railroad Pamphlet, n.d.).

The currently active Medicine Bow (Snowy Range) Ski Area, located on the south side of Route 130 above Hanging Lake, was opened in 1960 by Gaylord Wetherill and Edward Stratemeier of Kansas City (Wiegand 1976:79). It is the only functioning ski area in the Medicine Bow National Forest at this time (Terry Hoffman, Personal Communication 1981).

XIV.

WATER

The Forest as Watershed

THE MEDICINE BOW NATIONAL FOREST lies within the watersheds of the North Platte and Green Rivers. All waters west of the Continental Divide (the western portion of the Sierra Madres) flow into the Green River, thence into northwestern Colorado, and ultimately to the Pacific Ocean. The rest of the forest east of the Continental Divide drains into the North Platte River, thence to the Missouri River. There are approximately eight hundred miles of perennial streams and eighty lakes on the Medicine Bow National Forest, and water quality is assessed as excellent (USFS Management Situations 1980:4).

One of the most important functions of a forest is to protect watersheds. The importance of water as a resource was recognized early in the settlement of this region because of the semi-arid nature of most of the land. John H. Mullison, one of the first rangers in the forest, believed that water conservation would, in the long run, prove to be the most important result of maintaining a forest (Bruce 1959:29). Local residents realized that lack of water conservation would destroy the economic value of their property. Drainages from the forest furnished irrigation water for nearby stock raising ranches. The combination of summer range within the forest and the hay raised under irrigation made a stable local livestock industry possible (Armstrong 1935:27).

Early Forest Supervisor P. S. Lovejoy (1908–1911) realized that timber had a very marked effect on runoff, conserving and regulating the water flow. The relatively easy grades of the slopes allowed for slow runoff with little erosion and made tie-driving possible (Bruce 1959:28). Apparently the west slope of the Hayden presented the only serious erosion problem. Parts of that area were denuded from old slashings, fires and overgrazing, much of which occurred before the formation of the forest. Floods caused by spring runoffs were causing erosion; ranchers on the Little Snake were getting too much water in the spring and too little in the summer (Bruce 1959:38).

According to James Blackhall, long-term supervisor of the Hayden Division of the Sierra Madres, irrigation on lands adjacent to the forest began about 1880, consisting of small ditches to irrigate bottom lands. Almost all of the water from the Hayden, except for the North Platte, was appropriated for private irrigation concerns (Blackhall 1915:13).

A number of projects involving reservoirs, flumes, and ditches were undertaken in and around the Medicine Bow National Forest beginning in the late 1800s. Irrigation activity

Medicine Bow Collection — American Heritage Center
Stocking of streams by the Forest Service helps account for the high quality of fishing in the Medicine Bows; above; Ranger Williams plants trout in a high mountain stream.

increased in the late 1880s, as ranchers and small companies began acquiring water rights. Water and irrigation companies were established to handle various water schemes, providing storage and canals, and selling the water to users.

The Laramie Water Company was very active during these years in the Medicine Bows. Around 1908–1909, a project called the Bell Supply Ditch No. 2 was established from Douglas Creek below the mouth of Hay Creek, crossing the drainage of Beaver Spring and Muddy Creek. It terminated on the divide between Muddy Creek and the South Fork of the Little Laramie River. This project was surveyed by E. R. Pollock in 1908, and approved for flood water in 1909 by Clarence Johnson, state engineer. This was a collaboration between R. D. Stewart, the engineer for the Laramie, North Park and Western Railroad, and "Colonel" Edwin J. Bell, who controlled a great deal of rangeland in the Little Laramie drainage. The object was to divert water from the upper Douglas to the Little Laramie, create a reservoir in the Centennial Valley, and take the water out of the Little Laramie by means of a canal.

The water rights of the Laramie Water Company depended largely upon flood waters. The old Pioneer Ditch Company had some prior water rights, but transferred a sufficient amount to the Laramie Water Company to operate the Lake Hattie Reservoir. Lake Hattie was constructed between 1900–1910, and was supplied by a canal from Sodergreen Lake.

Ranger Louis E. Coughlin observed the serious erosion caused by the inefficient engineering of some of these early water projects. He also recognized the negative effects from the Lake Hattie project, noting severe erosion on the divide between Sodergreen Flats and the Lake Hattie Basin. His feeling was that it was fortunate that the Wyoming Development Company, which operated the Wheatland Reservoir, had prior water rights, preventing companies from developing and promoting much land in the vicinity of the Medicine Bow National Forest (Medicine Bow Collection).

Water for Cheyenne

The main water-related project in the Medicine Bow Forest at present is the Cheyenne or Snowy Range water diversion project, designed to provide a definite water supply for the city of Cheyenne until the year 2020, when its population is estimated to reach about 115,000 and will demand some 23 million gallons per day (*Wyoming State Tribune* 9/24/64).

The basic plan involved diverting water from Douglas Creek, a tributary of the North Platte, to Cheyenne, and repaying that water by diverting unappropriated water from the tributaries of the Little Snake River, west of the Continential Divide, into the Encampment and North Platte Rivers (*Laramie Daily Boomerang* 6/3/62).

The project covers eighty-three miles and crosses the Sierra Madre Range, the Snowy Range, and the Laramie Range — the present Hayden, Brush Creek, and Laramie Districts. Banner and Associates of Laramie were the surveyors and engineers for the project. Construction began in 1962, and Hog Park and Rob Roy reservoirs were completed by the end of 1965. Banner used a new type of steel tubing developed in the early 1950s capable of withstanding powerful internal pressure. The pipe system permitted a gravity flow across rugged terrain without a pump by having the point of the water's origin and each successive hilltop lower in elevation than the preceding point (*Wyoming State Tribune* 9/22/64). This use of gravity flow for over fifty miles from Douglas Creek to Middle Crow Creek saved Cheyenne nearly $500 thousand a year on pumping operations (*Wyoming State Tribune* 9/23/64).

The westernmost part of the project involves the Little Snake Diversion Pipeline and Hog Park Reservoir. A thirty-six-inch diameter, reinforced concrete pipeline collects water from the North Fork of the Little Snake and its tributaries west of the Continental Divide by means of several diversion dams, and from small streams and runoff. This water is transported under the Continental Divide to Hog Creek and Reservoir through a 3,480-foot long tunnel (Conner 1981:4).

Hog Creek Reservoir was completed in November 1965 to control channel erosion in Hog Park Creek (Timothy R. Conner, personal communication, 1981). Water released from Hog Park Reservoir into the North Platte River drainage is adjusted to balance the water removed from that drainage by the Douglas Creek diversions. Hog Park Reservoir has become a popular recreation site in the Sierra Madres, being large enough to accommodate canoes and other small boats (Conner 1981:5).

Rob Roy Reservior was completed on December 1965 and constitutes one of the chief permanent features of the system, Rob Roy is the main regulating reservoir, and impounds and regulates the flow of Douglas Creek. Water is released into Douglas Creek through a gated outlet tunnel and an ungated spillway at the west abutment of the dam. Rob Roy Reservoir is a major recreational attraction of the Medicine Bows, offering boating, camping, and picnicking (Conner 1981:5).

Water is then carried from small diversion dams on Douglas Creek and Horse Creek into Lake Owen by means of an eleven-mile, reinforced concrete pipeline. This pipeline discharges its water into the Lake Owen Reservoir, a natural lake enlarged to a capacity of 750-acre-feet by a small earthfill dam. Lake Owen serves to regulate water as well as reduce pressure between the Douglas Creek–Lake Owen pipeline and the Lake Owen–Middle Crow Creek pipeline (Conner 1981:5).

The next component in the system is a thirty-nine-mile pipeline from Lake Owen to Middle Crow Creek. The water flows by gravity through the pipeline, which empties into Middle Crow below the Vedauwoo Picnic Ground. It is then stored in reservoirs outside the forest (Granite Springs and Crystal Lake) owned by Cheyenne (Conner 1981:5).

In essence, as a result of this project, Cheyenne can draw out twelve million gallons per day from the North Platte, and simultaneously divert the same amount back into the Platte (*Wyoming State Tribune* 9/21/64).

Conclusion

There is convincing evidence that human groups had adapted to the mountains and foothills of the northwestern plains by late Paleo-Indian times. This way of living continued until historic times, but the degree of cultural continuity is unknown. Evidence from the Front Range suggests the mountain areas were affected by climatic changes and population fluctuations like the plains environment. There seem to have been migrations into the high country and periods of abandonment, and certain mountain areas seem to have been occupied during particular periods, while others were not. The high country of northwestern Wyoming was occupied throughout the Altithermal, while the record of occupation from the Colorado Front Range during the early Altithermal is absent.

Both the mountains of northern Wyoming and the Colorado Front Range have produced evidence of extensive occupation in the higher elevations. So far, the mountain areas of southern Wyoming have produced evidence of only limited use. Whether this reflects the actual pattern of prehistoric occupation or a lack of recorded sites is unknown.

By historic times, reports indicate the lower areas of the region were being extensively used by the Indians. Numerous tribes from widely scattered areas are reported to have hunted and raided in the region, which had a well-deserved reputation as dangerous country. Only hunting parties willing to expose themselves to the risk of enemy attack could take advantage of the abundant game. Since the early, written reports concerning the region came primarily from travelers who stayed in the lower country, little is known of the actual use historic tribes were making of the mountains. There were also few recorded observations made during the winter. Occasional mention of Indians hunting and gathering in the mountains, and war parties traveling through the region during winter is all that is recorded. The historic tribes using the area usually preferred to hunt the buffalo and were adjusted to life on the plains and intermountain basins, so their involvement in the high country was probably limited. The Utes and Shoshone made greater use of the mountains than others, but this may have been more a defensive measure than economic adaptation.

The significance of the Medicine Bow region in the history of Wyoming and western America lay in its abundant natural resources in close proximity to the transcontinental railroad and other major nineteenth century migration routes. The management and preservation of those precious resources became the responsibility of the United States Forest Service at the opening of the twentieth century.

Although logging, grazing, and limited mining are still conducted on the forest, emphasis has shifted in recent times to its recreational value to the general public. The high mountain lakes and streams, rugged rocky peaks, and endless vistas of forest and plain provide a last refuge — a physical and psychological release from twentieth century pressures heightened by fears of nuclear disaster, rampant pollution, and overpopulation of our sphere. For a short time at least, we can escape to a place the early explorers and the mountain men might still recognize, a place to rest one's overloaded senses and imagine a simpler way of life that has somehow escaped twentieth century man.

BIBLIOGRAPHY

Armstrong, Paul L.
History of the Medicine Bow National Forest Service. Manuscript on file, Wyoming State Archives and Historical Department, Historical Research and Publications Division, Cheyenne, Wyo., 1935.

Barnhart, William R.
The early history of Carbon County, Wyoming. Unpublished M.A. thesis, Department of History, University of Wyoming, Laramie Wyo., 1969.

Beard, Frances.
Wyoming from Territorial Days to the Present (Vol. 1). American Historical Society, Chicago and New York, 1933.

Beeler, H. C.
Mineral and allied resources of Albany County, Wyoming and vicinity. Laramie, Wyo: The Republican Press, 1906.

Beery, Gladys.
Report on evaluation of Echo Lodge. Manuscript on file, Medicine Bow National Forest, at Supervisor's Office, Laramie, Wyo. (no date).

Benedict, James B., and Olson, B. L.
The Mount Albion complex. Research report No. 1, Center for Mountain Archaeology, Ward, Colo., 1978.

Blackhall, James.
Hayden, Information. Manuscript on file, Medicine Bow National Forest Collection, American Heritage Center, University of Wyoming, Laramie, Wyo., 1915.

Bratt, John.
Trails of Yesterday. Lincoln, Chicago, and Dallas: The University Publishing Company, 1921.

Bruce, Robert K.
History of the Medicine Bow National Forest 1902–1910. Unpublished Master's Thesis, Department of History, University of Wyoming, Laramie, Wyo., 1959.

Burns, Robert H., Gillespie, Andrew S., and Richardson, Willing G.
Wyoming's Pioneer Ranches. Laramie, Wyo.: Top of the World Press, 1955.

Carter, Harvey L.
Dear Old Kit: The Historical Christopher Carson. Norman, Okla.: University of Oklahoma Press, 1968.

Chadey, Michael.
History in the making: Forest Service policy in regards to the restoration of the Snowy Range Lodge. Manuscript on file, Albany County Library, Laramie, Wyo., 1979.

Clark, William P.
The Indian sign language. Philadelphia: L. R. Hamersby, 1885.

Connor, Tim.
Project description: stage II water project. Report on file at Banner and Associates, Laramie, Wyo., 1981.

Cookson, David A.
Basques in Wyoming. In *Peopling the High Plains: Wyoming's European heritage,* edited by George O. Henrickson, pp. 95–120. Wyoming State Archives and Historical Department, Cheyenne, Wyo., 1977.

Coutant, C. G.
The History of Wyoming. Laramie, Wyo.: Chaplin, Spafford and Mathison, 1889.

————. The Rudefeha. (Coutant's Unpublished Notes), *Annals of Wyoming* 19(2):117–124. Publ., 1947.

Currey, D. R.
The Keystone gold-copper prospect area, Albany County, Wyo., *The Geological Survey of Wyoming, Preliminary Report No. 3,* Laramie, Wyo., 1965.

Dale, Harrison C. (editor).
The Ashley-Smith Explorations and the Discovery of a Central Route to the Pacific 1822–1829. Glendale, Calif.: Arthur H. Clark, 1941.

Dodge, Grenville M.
How We Built the Union Pacific Railway and Other Railway Papers and Addresses. Washington, D.C.: U.S. Government Printing Office, 1910.

Dodge, Richard I.
The Plains of the Great West (1959 ed.). New York: Archer House, 1877.

Duthie, George A.
The Medicine Bow National Forest, 1913–1916. Manuscript on file, Medicine Bow National Forest Collection, American Heritage Center, University of Wyoming, Laramie, Wyo., 1916.

Fremont, Bvt. Capt. John C.
Report of the exploring expedition to the Rocky Mountains. Washington, D.C.: Gales and Seaton, 1845.

Frison, George C.
Prehistoric Hunters of the High Plains. New York: Academic Press, 1978.

Goetzmann, William H.
Army exploration in the American West, 1803–1863. New Haven, Conn.: Yale University Press, 1966.

Grasso, Dennis N.
Physiography of the Medicine Bow National Forest. In *A Cultural Resouce Overview of the Medicine Bow National Forest and Thunder Basin National Grassland,* Vol. I. On file, Medicine Bow National Forest, Laramie, Wyo., 1982.

Hafen, Leroy.
The overland mail, 1849–1869. Cleveland, Ohio: Arthur H. Clark, 1926.

————. Fraeb's last fight and how Battle Creek got its name. *The Colorado Magazine* 7(3):97–101.

Hausel, W. Dan.
Gold Districts in Wyoming. *The Geological Survey of Wyoming, Report of Investigations No. 23,* Laramie, Wyo., 1980.

Hess, F. L.
Platinum Near Centennial, Wyo. *U.S. Geological Survey Bulletin No. 780-C,* pp. 127–135. Publ., 1926.

Hollenback, Frank R.
The Laramie Plains Line. Denver: Sage Books, 1960.

Homsher, Lola M.
The History of Albany County, Wyoming, to 1880. Unpublished Master's Thesis, Department of History, University of Wyoming, Laramie, Wyo., 1949.

Hyde, George H.
Indians of the High Plains. Norman, Okla.: University of Oklahoma Press, 1959.

Junge, Mark.
Grand Encampment Mining District. National Register Nomination, on file at Wyoming Recreation Commission, Cheyenne, Wyo., 1972.

————. Snowy Range Lodge. National Register Nomination, on file at Wyoming Recreation Commission, Cheyenne, Wyo., 1976.

Kennedy, J. C.
Carbon County Copper. *Annals of Wyoming* 2(3):69–72. Dated 1925.

Kerr, Corrine and Tom Rudkin.
Echo Lodge report. Manuscript on file, Medicine Bow National Forest, Supervisor's Office, Laramie, Wyo., 1979.

Knight, W. L.
Notes on the mineral resources of the state. *University of Wyoming Experimental Station Bulletin* 14. University of Wyoming, Laramie, Wyo. 1893.

Larson, T. A.
History of Wyoming. Lincoln, Nebr.: University of Nebraska Press, 1965.

Leonard, Peg L.
Wyoming, LaBonte County, 1820–1972. Lakeville, Mass.: Cranberry Press, 1972.

Linn, George B.
The tie drivers of the twenties. *In Wyoming,* April/May, 1973.

Lovejoy, P. S.
Report for Forest Atlas. (Administrative), Manuscript on file, Medicine Bow National Forest Collection, American Heritage Center, University of Wyoming, Laramie, Wyo., 1909.

McCallum, M.E., and Orback, C.J.
The New Rambler copper-gold-platinum district, Albany and Carbon counties, Wyoming. *Wyoming Geological Survey, preliminary report number 8.* Wyoming Geological Survey, Laramie, Wyo., 1968.

Medicine Bow National Forest Collection.
Account number 3654, American Heritage Center, University of Wyoming, Laramie, Wyo. Note: this collection is composed of 35 boxes of Forest Service records containing memoranda, correspondence, notes, reports, and photographs with an index.

Mullison, John H.
Report for Forest Atlas. (History), Manuscript on file, Medicine Bow National Forest Collection, American Heritage Center, University of Wyoming, Laramie, Wyo., 1909.

Mullison, John H., and Lovejoy, P. S.
History of the Cheyenne National Forest. Manuscript on file, Medicine Bow National Forest Collection, Box 11, American Heritage Center, University of Wyoming, Laramie, Wyo., 1909.

Osterwald, F. W., Osterwald, D.B., Long, Jr., J. S., and Wilson, W. H.
Mineral resources of Wyoming. *The Geological Survey of Wyoming, Bulletin No. 50,* Laramie, Wyo., 1966.

Parkman, Francis.
The Oregon Trail (1931 ed.). New York: Rinehart, 1849.

Peryam, E. C.
Indians and old trails. Newspaper clipping, Nov. 29, 1934, Medicine Bow National Forest Collection, Box 5, American Heritage Center, University of Wyoming, Laramie, Wyo., 1934.

Pinkerton, Joan T.
Knights of the Broadax: The Story of the Wyoming Tie Hacks, Caldwell, Idaho: The Caxton Printers, Ltd., 1981.

Potts, J. M.
Memorandum covering the past history, present organization and status and probable future of the Carbon Timber Company. Manuscript on file, Medicine Bow National Forest Collection, American Heritage Center, University of Wyoming, Laramie, Wyo., 1912.

Ratliff
Range management policy statement, Snake River Grazing District. Manuscript on file, Medicine Bow National Forest Collection, American Heritage Center, University of Wyoming, Laramie, Wyo., 1935.

Rusling, James F.
Across America: Or the Great West and the Pacific Coast. New York: Sheldon and Company, 1875.

Segerstrom, Kenneth, and Weisner, Robert C.
Mineral resources of the Laramie Peak study area, Albany and Converse Counties, Wyoming. *U.S. Geological Survey Bulletin 1397-B.* Washington, D.C.: U.S. Government Printing Office, 1977.

Smith, Duane
Rocky Mountain Mining Camps: the Urban Frontier. Bloomington, Ind.: Indiana University Press, 1967.

Spencer, A. C.
The Copper Deposits of the Encampment District. *U.S. Geological Survey Professional Paper No. 25.* Washington, D.C.: U.S. Government Printing Office, 1904.

———. Economic geology of the North Laramie Mountains, Converse and Albany Counties. Washington, D.C.: *U.S. Geological Survey Bulletin 626:* 47–81, dated 1916.

Stansbury, Captain Howard.
Exploration and survey of the valley of the Great Salt Lake of Utah *Senate Executive Document* No. 3, Special Session, March 1851. Philadelphia: Lippincott, Granbo, 1852.

———. *Exploration and survey of the valley of the Great Salt Lake of Utah.* U.S. Engineer Department (published by order of the House of Representatives), Robert Armstrong, Washington, 1853.

Thompson, Robert L.
Wiring A Continent: The History of the Telegraph Industry in the United States, 1832–1866. Princeton, N.J.: Princeton University Press, 1947.

Toll, Oliver W.
Arapaho Names and Trails. Privately printed. On file, Rocky Mountain National Park, Estes Park, Colo., 1962.

U.S., Congress, House.
Message From the President of the United States to the two Houses of Congress (Report of Lt. F. T. Bryan). 35th Congress, First Session, Vol. 943, *H.R. Exec. Doc.2,* Cornelius Wendell, printer, Washington, 1857.

————. Messages and Documents, War Department (Wagon-Road in Wyoming). 49th Congress, Third Session, Vol. 2/Part 3, *House Ex. Doc. No. 253,* Washington, D.C.: U.S. Government Printing Office, 1879.

U.S., Congress, Senate.
Diary of a trip from Fort Bridger, Utah Territory, via Bridger's Pass and Laramie Plain to Fort Laramie, Nebraska Territory, by Mr. John Bartleson. 35th Congress, Second Session, and Special Session, of the Senate of 1859, Vol. 975 *Sen. Exec. Doc. 1,* William A. Harris, Printer, Washington, 1859.

————. Testimony as to the claim of Ben Holladay. 46th Congress, Second Session, Vol. No. 1890, *Senate Miscellaneous Doc. 19.* GPO, Washington, 1880.

U.S. Forest Service.
Management stipulations, Medicine Bow National Forest. Manuscript on file, Supervisor's Office, Laramie, Wyo., 1980.

U.S. War Department.
Report on barracks and hospitals: Fort Steele. *Surgeon General's Office Circular No. 4.* Washington, D.C.: U.S. Government Printing Office, 1870.

Vass, A. F., and Pearson, Harry.
An economic study of range sheep production on the Red Desert and adjoining areas. *Agricultural Experiment Station Bulletin 156.* Laramie, Wyo.: University of Wyoming, 1927.

Wentworth, Edward N.
America's sheep trails. Ames, Iowa: Iowa State College Press, 1948.

Wiegand, Catherine (editor)
Centennial, Wyoming, 1876–1976: The Real Centennial. Denver, Colo.: Silers Printing Company, 1976.

Wright, Gary A., Bender, Susan and Reeve, Stuart.
High country adaptations. *Plains Anthropologist* 25(89): 181–197.
Publ. 1980.

Writer's Project.
Wyoming: A Guide to its History, Highways and People. New York:
Oxford University Press, 1941.

APPENDIX

FOREST SUPERVISORS OF THE MEDICINE BOW NATIONAL FOREST
(Medicine Bow Collection)

Davis, Lewis G.	1903–1907
Nelson, Jesse W.	1907–1908
Lovejoy, Parish S.	1908–1911
Granger, Christopher M.	1911–1913
Duthie, George A.	1913–1917
Pierce, Earl S.	1916(?)–1920
Hilton, Huber C.	1921–1934
Woodhead, Phillip V.	1934–1935
Veeder, Jarvis S.	1935–1942
Averill, Clarence C.	1943–1948
Nordwall, David S.	1948–1950
Fortenberry, E. J.	1951–1957
Brown, G. K.	1957–1960
Augsbach, William E.	1961–1973
Bennett, John E.	1973–1974
Duhncrack, Alan R.	1974–1976
Rollens, Donald L.	1976–1982
O'Neal, Sonny	1983–present
Blackhall, James (Hayden N. F.)	1908–1928

INDEX

— A —

Acme Consolidated Gold & Copper Mining Co., 99
Albany, 70,137
Albany County, 45, 61, 126, 127, 128,136
Albion Mine, 101
Altithermal, 3, 161
Anderson, F. E., 100
Apache Indians, 20
Arapaho Indians, xx, 6, 8, 15, 17, 18, 22, 24, 25, 26, 28, 29, 30, 41
Archaic Period, 4
Arikara Indians, 20
Arlington, 99, 122, 130
Arundell, Benjamin W., 97
Ashley, William H., 12, 25, 26, 34, 35, 37

— B —

Baker, Jim, 16, 28, 37
Banner and Associates, 159
Barber Lake Road, 127, 146, 154
Barrett Creek, 72, 73, 142, 148
Barrett Ridge, 143, 144, 153, 154
Bartleson, John, 40
Basin Land and Livestock Company, 115
Basque sheepherders, 116, 120, 121
Battle, 107, 108, 133
Battle Creek, 9, 36
Battle Lake, 108, 136
The Battle Miner, 107
Battle Mountain, 37
Beaver Spring, 158
Bell, Edwin J., 158
Bell Supply Ditch No. 2, 158
Bergstrom Brothers, 69

Big Five Mine, 112
Big Laramie River, 128, 130, 136
Big Laramie Stage Station, 40
Bitter Creek, 38
Blackfeet Indians, 8, 33
Blackhall, James, 53, 114, 157
Black's Fork, 37
Black Mountain, 135
Boston-Wyoming Copper Company, 112
Boswell Ranch, 128, 129
Box Elder Creek, 135
Bridger, Jim, 6, 7, 36, 37, 38
Bridger Mine, 104
Bridger's Pass, 38, 39, 40
Bridger's Pass Stage Station, 41
Brooklyn Lake, 52, 53, 115, 126, 130, 151, 154
Brooklyn Lodge, 151
Brown, Charles H., 57
Brush Creek, 52, 61, 67, 94, 99, 126, 142
Bryan, Lt. Francis T., 39
Buford, 44
Bunnell, Edwin, 86
Burns, Otto L., 100
Bussard, Charley, 60

— C —

Cache la Poudre River, 30, 36, 40, 60
California gold rush, 30
Camp Herman, 101
Carbon, 99, 130
Carbon County, 136
Carbon Timber Company, 52, 63, 64, 65, 66, 67, 68, 70, 71, 76, 84, 133
Carlson Creek, 131
Carson, Kit, 33, 34, 35, 36

Cedar Creek Corrals, 117
Centennial, 52, 74, 103, 117, 122, 126, 127, 136, 137, 146, 151, 152
Centennial Commercial Club, 126
Centennial Gold Mining Company, 102
Centennial Mine, 101, 102
Centennial-Snowy Range Wagon Road, 126
Central Pacific Railroad, 44
Ceramics, 21
Charlie Mine, 101
Charter Oak Mine, 104
Cherokee Indians, 30, 37, 40
Cherokee Trail, 17, 30, 31, 122
Cheyenne, 124, 159
Cheyenne Indians, 6, 7, 17, 18, 25, 28, 38, 41
Cheyenne Pass, 38
Cheyenne Pass Road, 124
Cheyenne and Northern Railroad, 59
Cheyenne Water Diversion Project, 159
Chicago, Burlington & Quincy Railroad, 59
Chicago Copper Refining Company, 105
Chimney Park, 49, 129
Civilian Conservation Corps, 54, 92, 107, 131, 139–145
Civilan Conservation Corps Camps
  Arlington, 141
  Brush Creek, 141, 144, 154
  Centennial, 141, 144
  Chimney Park, 141, 142, 144
  Encampment, 141
  Esterbrook, 141, 144
  French Creek, 141
  Mullen Creek, 141, 144, 145, 155
  Pole Mountain, 141, 144, 155
  Ryan Park, 141, 142, 144
  Saratoga, 141, 143, 144, 154
Clark, Captain, W. P., xx
Coalmont, 136, 137, 138
Cody Complex, 2
Coe and Carter, 60, 61, 62, 63, 80
Coe and Coe, 63
Colby Site, 1
Colorado, Wyoming and Eastern Railroad, 137

Comanche Indians, 20
Como, 44
Cooper Creek Stage Station, 40
Cooper Hill Deep Mining Company 101
Cooper Hill Mines, 101
Cooper Lake, 44
Copper, 94, 95, 97, 101, 102, 104, 105, 107, 110, 111, 112
Copper Creek, 104
Copper King Mine, 112
Copperton, 107, 108, 133
Corps of Topographical Engineers, 32, 35, 37
Cosgriff Brothers, 114
Cottonwood Creek, 135
Coughlin, Louis E., 49, 50, 53, 70, 158
Coutant, C. G., xix
Creighton, Edward, 55
Crismore, Charles, 152
Crook, General George, 17
Crow Creek, 38
Crow Indians, 7, 18, 25
Crystal Lake Dam, 160
Cullerton, Ben, 104

— D —

Dale Creek, City, 44
Daley, William W., 113
Daniels and Helmick, 72
Davis, Lewis G., 49, 50
Dawson Brothers, 60
Days, 127
Deal, Robert, 105
Deep Creek-Fireline Trail, 116
Devils Gate, 65
Dillon, 107, 108, 109, 133
The Dillon Double Jack, 109
Dillon, Malachi, 109
Doane, George, 104
Doane-Rambler Mine, 104, 107, 108, 132
Dodge, Grenville M., 43, 44, 152
Doll, Raymond and Bernice, 150
Douglas, Captain, 93
Douglas Creek, 61, 66, 71, 72, 73, 74, 75, 85, 93, 94, 95, 149, 151, 158, 159, 160
Douglas Creek Tie Camp Company, 70

Douglas Mine, 95
Downey, Col. Stephen W., 99, 102
Duran, Thomas, 44
Duthie, George A., 53
Dutton Creek, 72

— E —

Eagle Peak Truck Trail, 144
Echo Lodge (Roper Place), 149, 150, 151
Egolf, David, 147
Elk Mountain, 31, 35, 36, 38, 39, 40, 42, 58, 59, 132
Elkhorn Driveway, 116
Elk Mountain Stage Station, 40
Elwood, 107
Elwood, Tom, 107
Emerson, Willis George, 105
Emma G. Mine, 101
Encampment (Grand Encampment), 67, 107, 110, 111, 130, 132, 133, 134, 136
Encampment Meadows, 133
Encampment River, 18, 67, 106, 132, 133, 159
Encampment-Slater Driveway, 116
Engstrom, Charles, 70
Ernest, Boney, 104
Esterbrook, 112
Evans, Captain Lewis, 30, 37

— F —

Fairview Mine, 99
Ferris, George, 105
Ferris-Haggarty Copper Mining Co., 105
Ferris-Haggarty (Rudefeha) Mine, 104, 105, 106, 107, 108, 109, 110, 132, 133
Fetterman Massacre, 42
Finfrock, Dr. J. H., 42
Fire Lookouts, 50, 87–92, 144
Fitzpatrick, Tom, 35, 36
Five Buttes, 37
Florence Mine, 95
Fort Bridger, 37, 38, 39, 40
Fort Fetterman, 134, 135
Fort Fetterman and Rock Creek Stage Road, 134, 135
Fort Halleck, 42, 58

Fort Jackson, 37
Fort Phil Kearney, 33
Fort Laramie (Fort William), 7, 13, 28, 35, 39, 40, 55, 135
Fort McKinney, 134
Fort D. A. Russell (Fort F. E. Warren), Target & Maneuver Reservation, 47, 48, 124
Fort St. Vrain, 35
Fort Sanders, 17, 42, 43, 44, 59, 60
Fort (Fred) Steele, 58, 62, 64, 67, 72, 75, 84, 85, 93, 105, 114, 132
Fort F. E. Warren, 140
Fortymile Ranch, 135
Fourmile Creek, 131
Foxpark, 53, 68, 69, 70
Foxpark Tie and Timber Workers Union, 80
Foxpark Timber Company, 68, 70, 74, 77
Fraeb, Henry, 28, 36, 37, 107
Fraeb's Fort, 8, 9
Free Gold Mine, 102
Fremont, John C., 8, 26, 30, 35, 36, 37, 38
French Creek, 18, 49, 61, 86
  South French Creek, 61, 90
  North French Creek, 67

— G —

Gilman and Carter, 59, 60
Godoy, Alexis, 36
Gold, 93, 94, 95, 96, 97, 100, 101, 102, 104, 111, 112
Gold Hill, 97, 99, 100, 101, 126, 130, 136
Gore, Sir George, 93
Gramm, 69, 70
Gramm, Otto, 68, 70
Grand Encampment Herald, 67
Grand River Valley Railroad, 136
Granger, Christopher M., 52, 87
Granite Springs Dam, 160
Grant, Mortimer N., 130
Grazing Homestead Law of 1916, 49
Green Mountain, 133, 134
Green Rock Picnic Ground, 152
Gros Ventre Indians, 9, 20, 36

— H —

Hadsell, Frank, 113
Haggarty Creek, 108
Haggarty, Ed, 104, 105
Hanna, 71, 114
Happy Jack Road, 124
Happy Jack Ski Area, 155
Hay Creek, 158
Hayden, Dr. F. V., 47, 93
Haystack Flats, 38
Hickman, Lewis, xx
Hilton, Huber C., 53, 54, 150
Hitchcock, W. A., 146
Hog Park, 64, 67, 130, 133, 134
Hog Park Reservoir, 159, 160
Hogpark Trail, 116
Holladay, Ben, 39, 40, 41, 42, 55, 58
Hollingsworth, Jack, 124
Holmes, 71, 93, 102
Holmes-Laramie Stage Line, 133
Hoover, President Herbert, 47
Horse Creek, 71, 160
Hotel de Maine, 107
Hull, A. J., 103
Huston, Al, 104
Hutton, C. H., 58
Hutton, Charley, 60

— I —

Indian Creek, 72
Influenza epidemic, 86
Inspiration Point Ski Area, 154, 155

— J —

Jack Creek, 9, 24, 122, 133
Jelm, 130
Johnston, Col. Albert S., 40
Johnson, Clarence, 158
Jones, Grant, 109
Jones, Harry, 151
Julesburg, Colorado, 28, 40, 41

— K —

Keystone, 52, 53, 66, 71, 72, 76, 96,
    130, 150
Keystone Mine, 95
Kindt, Fred, 113, 114
Kiowa Indians, 20
Knight, Dr. S. H., 153

Kurtze Chatterton Mine, 104

— L —

Lake Creek, 122
Lake Hattie, 158
Lake Marie, 126, 154
Lake Owen, 160
Lambing, I. P., 102
La Bonte, 35
    La Bonte Canyon, 92
    La Bonte Creek, 111
La Plata, 126
La Prele Creek, 111, 134
La Ramie, Jacque, 25, 33
Laramie, 17, 44, 45, 60, 68, 70, 72,
    74, 99, 124, 126, 127, 128, 129,
    131, 136 137, 138, 146, 155
Laramie-Gold Hill Road, 130
Laramie, Hahns Peak and Pacific Rail-
    road, 52, 53, 68, 100, 103, 126,
    136, 137, 138
Laramie, North Park and Pacific Rail-
    road, 136
Laramie, North Park and Western
    Railroad Company, 137, 158
Laramie Peak, 9, 29, 57, 58
    mining, 111, 112, 135
Laramie Plains, 6, 7, 12, 13, 18, 20,
    21, 22, 26, 28, 30, 33, 34, 36,
    38, 39, 40, 42, 44, 135
Laramie Plains Line, 136
Laramie Range, Mountains, xix, 11,
    12, 13, 15, 18, 20, 25, 28, 33,
    34, 35, 38, 39, 40, 43, 59, 124,
    134, 135
Laramie River, 6, 8, 25, 26, 28, 30,
    33, 36, 42, 60, 70, 74
Laramie Timber Company, 69
Laramie and Hahn's Peak Wagon
    Road, 134
Laramie Water Company, 158
Larimer and Routt County Railway
    Company, 137
Late Prehistoric Period, 4
Lead, 101, 104
Levon, R. M., 100
Lewis and Clark, 21
Libby Creek, 126, 127, 146
Libby Creek Ski Area, 144, 154
Libby Flats, 53, 126
Lincoln Highway, 144, 152, 155
Lindaley, Lorraine, 90, 91

Lisa, Manuel, 33
Little Ice Age, 10
Little Laramie River, 34, 60, 158
Little Laramie Stage Station, 40
Little Sandstone Creek, 108
Little Snake River, 9, 18, 24, 30, 36, 37, 131, 157, 159
Lodgepole Creek, 28, 29, 38, 39, 43, 44
Lodgepole Trail, 39, 42, 122, 124
Lookout, 44
Lovejoy, P. S., 52, 88, 118, 126, 156

— M —

McCaffery, Barnard, 105
McCool, J. S., 60
McFadden, 122
McKinley, President William, 46, 47
MacNeel, Dr. J. R., 143
Maggie Murphy Mine, 112
Marcy, Randolph B., 40
May, Claude, 148
Medicine Bow, 59, 62, 64, 135
Medicine Bow-Fort Fetterman Wagon Road, 135
Medicine Bow Lodge, 143, 148, 149, 153
Medicine Bow National Forest
  divisions and districts, 46–54
  formation of, 46–49, 64
  grazing, 113–119
  logging, 55–87
  mining, 93–112
  personnel, 49–54
  recreation, 146–155
  roads, 122–135
  watershed, 156–160
Medicine Bow Peak, 87, 88, 89, 90, 127, 152
Medicine Bow Range, Mountains, xix, xx, 13, 17, 20, 22, 26, 30, 31, 33, 34, 35, 36, 40, 62, 77, 84, 94, 114, 122
Medicine Bow River, 8, 28, 36, 39, 61, 62, 63, 64, 130, 117
Medicine Bow Ski Area, 155
Medicine Bow Stage Station, 40, 134
Meeker Massacre, 49
Meeker, Nathan, 24
Meyer, Louis R., 63, 64
Meyer, R. D., 64

Middle Crow Creek, 159, 160
Middle Fork Mill Creek, 130
Middle Plains Archaic Period, 4
Midway, 134
Mill Creek, 131
Miller, Fred, 88, 90
Miller, Ike, C., 113
Milo, 117
mining frontier urbanization, 106, 107
Miser, 44
Mizner, Captain Henry R., 42
Moore, Iram, 94
Moore's Gulch, 94
Mountain Home, 128, 140
Muddy Creek, 71, 142, 158
Muddy Creek Tie Camp, 150
Mullison, John H., 15, 16, 21, 33, 49, 53, 61, 62, 94, 156
Mullison Park, 94
Murdock, T. B., 58

— N —

Nash's Fork, 126, 127
National Register of Historical Places, 148, 153
Nelson, Jesse W., 50, 51, 52
Nelson, Osea, 69
New Rambler Mine, 97, 102, 130, 133
North American Copper Company, 110
North Cedar Creek, 113
North Fork Little Laramie, 126, 130
North Fork Main Mill Creek, 117
North Gate Canyon, 26
North Laramie River, 135
North Park, 128, 129, 131, 136, 137
North Platte River, 8, 18, 21, 22, 24, 25, 26, 30, 33, 35, 36, 38, 40, 55, 58, 62, 67, 75, 84, 114, 122, 126, 156, 157, 159, 160
North Platte Stage Station, 41
North Platte Valley, 124, 136
North Colorado and Eastern Railroad Company, 137
Norton, Jack Ranch, 120

— O —

Oberg Pass, 81
Old French Creek Road, 130

Old Sherman Road, 124
Olsen, 134
Olson, Andrew, 64, 70
Olson, Hans, 70
Opal, 114
Oregon Trail, 37, 40, 44, 55, 113
Oriole Mine, 112
Otto Lumber Company, 70, 74
Overland Mail, 39, 55, 58
Overland Stage, 28, 40, 41, 42
Overland Trail, 28, 30, 37, 40, 41, 42, 58, 122, 124

— P —

Pacific Railroad and Telegraph Company, 136
Paleo-Indian Period, xix, 1, 2, 3, 4
Parkman, Francis, xviii, 10, 13, 15
Pass Creek, 10, 31, 39, 67, 114, 124
Pass Creek Stage Station, 41
Pawnee Indians, 20, 28
Paxton and Turner, 59
Peace Commission of 1867, 42
Penn-Wyoming Copper Company, 110
Pinchot, Gifford, 49
Pine Grove Stage Station, 41
Pioneer Ditch Company, 158
Platinum, 94, 97, 102, 103
Platinum City, 103
Point of Rocks Station, 135
Pole Mountain, 50, 124, 140, 142, 143, 155
Pollock, E. R., 158
Pony Express, 55
Powder River country, 28
Promontory Point, 42
Pullum, John, 9
Pullam's Fork, 36
Purgatory Gulch, 104, 132
Pyramid Mine, 112

— R —

R. R. Crow and Company, 72, 73
Ralston Cabin, 115
Rambler, 107, 108, 133
Rambler Mining and Smelting Company, 97
Ranger Stations
  Big Creek, 52

Bow River, 53, 130
Brush Creek, 53
Centennial, 126, 145
Corral, 116
Fox Park, 52
Heather Creek, 52
Medicine Bow, 52
Rambler, 141
Trail, 116
Rawlins, 114, 133
Red Butte, 44
Red Cloud, 42
Red Desert, 21, 38, 113
Richmond Mine, 101
Rip Van Winkle Consolidated Company, 101
Riverside, 132
Riverside Ranch, 128
Rob Roy Reservoir, 159, 160
Rock Creek, 8, 10, 44, 59, 61, 63, 64, 74, 130
Rock Creek Stage Station, 40, 134, 135
Rock River, 72
Rock Springs, 114
Rocky Mountain Coal Company, 62
Rocky Mountain Fur Company, 37
Roper, Billy, 150
Rudefelha,, 133
Rumsey, John, 105
Ryan Park, 143, 148, 153

— S —

Sage Creek Stage Station, 41
Sage, Rufus, 8, 25, 31
Salt Lake Stage Road, 124
Sand Lake, 52, 101, 130, 151, 152
Sand Lake Resort, 151
Saratoga, 8, 15, 52, 72, 99, 107, 111, 127, 130, 133
Saratoga and Encampment Railroad, 110
Saratoga-Gold Hill Road, 117, 130
Sarpy, Peter, 37
Savage, Bill, 104
Savage Corrals, 117
Savage, Walter and Richard, 113
Savery Creek, 24, 36
Savery-Fireline Trail, 116
Schlotzer, Anthony "Pop", 147
Schnitzler, Jacob, 102

Scott, Dr. J. W., 152
Scribner Stage Company, 133
Sederlin, Louis, 62
Seminoe Mountains, 22
Sevenmile Creek, 131
Sheep Mountain, 47, 122, 144, 152
Sherman Camp Station, 44, 59, 60,
    124
Shoshone Indians, 6, 8, 11, 12, 17,
    18, 20, 21, 22, 23, 24, 28, 162
Sierra Madres, xix, 2, 6, 9, 18, 22,
    24, 28, 30, 36, 38, 40, 66, 84
    Mining, 104, 105, 106, 107,
        108, 109, 110, 111
    Grazing, 114, 116
    Roads, 131
    Watershed, 157
Silver, 101, 104, 112
Silver City, 9, 146, 148
Silver King Mine, 101
Sioux (Oglala) Indians, 6, 7, 10, 11,
    12, 13, 14, 15, 17, 18, 20, 22,
    28, 38, 41
Sisson and Moore, 148
Smith North Creek, 149
Snowy Range, 33, 60, 61, 84, 126,
    130, 136
Snowy Range Fishing Lodge, 152
Snowy Range (Libby) Lodge, 9, 146,
    147, 148, 154
Snowy Range Natural Area, 152
Snowy Range Road, 52, 54, 124,
    125, 126, 127, 151
Snowy Range Winter Sports Area,
    155
Snowy Range Winter Sports Club,
    154
Soda Lakes, 136
Sodergreen Lake, 158
Soldiers Road, 132
South Brush Creek Picnic Ground,
    144
South Pass, 36
South Platte River, 18, 25, 34, 35,
    37, 38, 40
South Pole Creek, 124
Southwick, J. W., 104
Spanish exploration, 32
Spotswood, Robert, 41
Sprague, Davis and Company, 59
Spring Creek, 133
Squaw Mountain, 37

Stanley Park, 117
Standard Timber Company, 68, 69
Stansbury, Captain Howard, xviii, 6,
    12, 13, 37, 38, 39, 40
Stephens, Captain, 13, 26
Stewart, R. D., 158
Stock driveways, 116
Strandquist, Victor, 70
Stratton, E., 116
Stroud and Sheppard, 70, 72
Stuart, Robert, 8, 25
Sulphur Springs Stage Station, 41
Summit Inn, 152, 155
Summit Ski Area, 152, 155
Sun, Tom, 104
Sweetwater River, 36
Sybille Creek, 25

— T —

Taylor Grazing Act, 119, 121
Taylor, Robert, 113
Telephone Canyon, 124
Telephone Creek Draw, 124
Telephone Road, 124
Teller, J. C., 67
Tennant Creek, 107
Tie Siding, 59, 60, 122
Thomson, Tommy and Edith, 150
Thompson Lodge, 151
Thornburgh, Major Thomas T., 24
Three Cripples Mine, 112
Tie City, 124
timber lodges, 9
Timber and Stone Act of 1878, 63, 64
Tomasek, Charles, 115
Towner lake, 142
Trabing Brothers, 60
tramp herding, 120
transcontinental telegraph, 55, 57, 58
transhumance, 116
Treaty of Fort Laramie, 7
Tupper, Clarence, 9
Turk Site, 1
Turpin Creek, 62, 92
Twin Groves, 122

— U —

Union Pacific Coal Company, 45, 64
Union Pacific Mammoth Site, 1

Union Pacific Railroad, 22, 28, 42, 43, 44, 45, 58, 59, 60, 61, 62, 63, 64, 66, 67, 68, 74, 77, 78, 81, 85, 113, 114, 124, 132, 133, 134, 137, 138, 148, 150, 151
Union Timber Company, 69
United Smelters, Railway & Copper Company, 110
University of the Wilderness, 153
University of Wyoming, 143, 145, 152, 153
University of Wyoming Summer Science Camp, 152, 153
U.S. Army, 28, 30
U.S. Army, 139, 140
U.S. Geological Survey, 102
Ute Indians, 6, 8, 10, 17, 18, 22, 24, 49, 94, 162
Utopia Mine, 102

— V —

Vagner, Charles L., 63
Van Horn, Isaac, 100, 136
Vedauwoo, 15, 142, 160
Vernon, Captain, 144
Virginia Dale, 41, 124

— W —

Walcott, 107, 110, 133

Walden, 128, 129
Warbonnet Mining district, 112
Warbonnet Peak, 111
Webber's Sawmill, 126
Webster, Cyril, 86,
Wetherill, Gaylord and Stratemeier, Edward, 155
White, Frank, 134
Wiant's Ranch, 117
Wilcox and Crout, 60
Will, William F., 53
Williams, Ezekial, 25, 33
Williams, Frank O., 104
Wilt, Dan, 68, 69
Windy Hill Road, 130
Wister, Owen, xix
Woods Landing, 128
Woods Landing-Mountain Home Road, 128
Woods, Sam, 129
Works Progress Administration, 144
Wyoming Central Railroad, 59
Wyoming Deveopment Co., 158
Wyoming Fish and Game Department, 142
Wyoming Platinum and Gold Mining Syndicate, 103
Wyoming Timber Company, 68, 70, 71, 72, 73, 75, 76, 86, 150